W

Re

for

AS

C

Gwynn ap Gwilym

Edited by Richard Gray

Illuminate
Publishing

Published in 2016 by Illuminate Publishing Ltd, P.O Box 1160, Cheltenham, Gloucestershire GL50 9RW

Orders: Please visit www.illuminatepublishing.com
or email sales@illuminatepublishing.com

This book is dedicated to the memory of Gwynn ap Gwilym, who sadly passed away shortly after its completion. It is a fitting tribute to a man who dedicated his life to the promotion of religious values. He will be greatly missed by all those who knew and worked with him. His humility, wit and good humour in the face of adversity were an example to us all. Hwyl fawr Gwynn.

British Library Cataloguing-in-Publication Data

A catalogue record for this book is available from the British Library

ISBN 978-1-908682-95-6

Printed by Barley Print, Cuffley Herts

3.18

The publisher's policy is to use papers that are natural, renewable and recyclable products made from wood grown in sustainable forests. The logging and manufacturing processes are expected to conform to the environmental regulations of the country of origin.

Every effort has been made to contact copyright holders of material reproduced in this book. If notified, the publishers will be pleased to rectify any errors or omissions at the earliest opportunity.

This material has been endorsed by WJEC/Eduqas and offers high quality support for the delivery of WJEC/Eduqas qualifications. While this material has been through a WJEC/Eduqas quality assurance process, all responsibility for the content remains with the publisher.

WJEC/Eduqas examination questions are reproduced by permission from WJEC/Eduqas

Series editor: Richard Gray
Editor: Geoff Tuttle
Design and Layout: EMC Design Ltd, Bedford

Acknowledgements

Cover Image: © Noronha Rui/iStock

Image credits:

p. 7 Durer [Public domain]; **p. 9** Antonio da Correggio [Public domain]; **p. 12** Public domain; **p. 20** Carvaggio [Public domain]; **p. 21** Witz [Public domain]; **p. 23** Dbleicher (Diskussion) (Self-photographed) [CC BY-SA 3.0 de (http://creativecommons.org/licenses/by-sa/3.0/de/deed.en), CC BY-SA 3.0 (http://creativecommons.org/licenses/by-sa/3.0) or GFDL (http://www.gnu.org/copyleft/fdl.html)], via Wikimedia Commons; **p. 24** Courtesy of Rt Revd Prof. N.T. Wright; **p. 31** Orrza; **p. 33** Nathan Holland; **p. 35** Juan de Flandes [Public domain], via Wikimedia Commons; **p. 41** Courtesy of Sallie McFague; **p. 43** © Basso Cannarsa/LUZphoto/Redux; **p. 49** Public domain; **p. 50** Fresco in Capella Sistina, Vatican [Public domain], via Wikimedia Commons; **p. 51** Licenced under the Creative Commons Attribution-Share Alike 3.0 license; **p. 52** Everett Collection Historical / Alamy Stock Photo; **p. 53** Public domain; **p. 58** William Holman Hunt [Public domain], via Wikimedia Commons: **p. 60** (top & bottom) Public domain; **p. 61** Public domain; **p. 64** Jastrow [CC BY 3.0 (http://creativecommons.org/licenses/by/3.0)], via Wikimedia Commons; **p. 68** Georgios Kollidas; **p. 70** Everett – Art; **p. 71** Courtesy of Scott Faber Photography; **p. 84** Artmig; **p. 85** Freedom Studio; **p. 86** Jacopo Amigoni [Public domain], via Wikimedia Commons; **p. 92** Antonio Gravante; **p. 93** Nicku; **p. 94** Jesus Army; **p. 95** Granger Historical Picture Archive/Alamy Stock Photo; **p. 101** Anneka; **p. 102** Maarzolino; **p. 108** Warren Bouton; **p. 109** Richard Pinder; **p. 113** Melchior2008 (Own work) [Public domain], via Wikimedia Commons

Contents

About this book

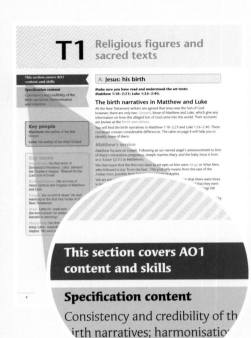

With the new A Level in Religious Studies, there is a lot to cover and a lot to do in preparation for the examinations at the end of AS or the full A Level. The aim of these books is to provide enough support for you to achieve success at AS and A Level, whether as a teacher or a learner.

This series of books is skills-based in its approach to learning, which means it aims to combine covering the content of the Specification with examination preparation from the start. In other words, it aims to help you get through the course whilst at the same time developing some important skills needed for the examinations.

To help you study, there are clearly defined sections for each of the AO1 and AO2 areas of the Specification. These are arranged according to the Specification Themes and use, as far as is possible, Specification headings to help you see that the content has been covered, for both AS and A Level.

The AO1 content is detailed, but precise, with the benefit of providing you with references to both religious/philosophical works and to the views of scholars. The AO2 responds to the issues raised in the Specification and provides you with ideas for further debate, to help you develop your own evaluation skills.

Ways to use this book

In considering the different ways in which you may teach or learn, it was decided that the books needed to have an inbuilt flexibility to adapt. As a result, they can be used for classroom learning, for independent work by individuals, as homework, and, they are even suitable for the purposes of 'flip learning' if your school or college does this.

You may be well aware that learning time is so valuable at A Level and so we have also taken this into consideration by creating flexible features and activities, again to save you the time of painstaking research and preparation, either as teacher or learner.

Features of the books

The books all contain the following features that appear in the margins, or are highlighted in the main body of the text, in order to support teaching and learning.

Key terms of technical, religious and philosophical words or phrases

> **Key terms**
>
> Holy Spirit: God as he is active in the world

Quickfire questions simple, straightforward questions to help consolidate key facts about what is being digested in reading through the information

> **quickfire**
>
> 1.1 Where do Matthew's Old Testament quotations come from?

Key quotes either from religious and philosophical works and/or the works of scholars

> **Key quote**
>
> I … decided, after investigating everything carefully from the very first, to write an orderly account. (Luke 1:3)

Study tips advice on how to study, prepare for the examination and answer questions

Study tip

Make sure that you do not confuse what Matthew says with what Luke says.

AO1 Activities that serve the purpose of focusing on identification, presentation and explanation, and developing the skills of knowledge and understanding required for the examination

AO1 Activity

Prepare a 30-second news flash on how Jesus' birth is presented in Matthew and a 30-second news flash on how Jesus' birth is presented in Luke.

This practises the AO1 skill of selecting and presenting the key relevant information.

AO2 Activities that serve the purpose of focusing on conclusions, as a basis for thinking about the issues, developing critical analysis and the evaluation skills required for the examination

AO2 Activity *Possible lines of argument*

Listed below are some conclusions that could be drawn from the AO2 reasoning in the accompanying text:

Glossary of all the key terms for quick reference.

Specific feature: Developing skills

This section is very much a focus on 'what to do' with the content and the issues that are raised. They occur at the end of each section, giving 12 AO1 examples and 12 AO2 examination-focused activities.

The Developing skills are arranged progressively, so as to provide initial support for you at first, and then gradually encourage you to have more independence.

AO1 and AO2 answers and commentaries

The final section has a selection of answers and commentaries as a framework for judging what an effective and ineffective response may be. The comments highlight some common mistakes and also examples of good practice so that all involved in teaching and learning can reflect upon how to approach examination answers.

Richard Gray
Series Editor
2016

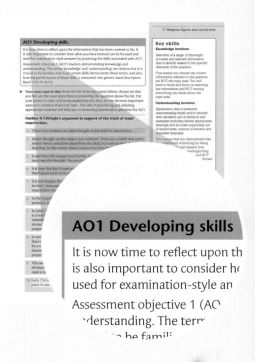

5

T1 Religious figures and sacred texts

This section covers AO1 content and skills

Specification content

Consistency and credibility of the birth narratives; harmonisation and redaction.

Key people

Matthew: the author of the first Gospel

Luke: the author of the third Gospel

Key terms

Benedictus: the first word of Zechariah's Prophecy; Latin: *blessed*; the Prophecy begins: 'Blessed be the Lord God of Israel'

Birth narratives: the account of Jesus' birth in the Gospels of Matthew and Luke

Gospel: the record of Jesus' life and teaching in the first four books of the New Testament

Magi: Latin for 'wise men' – originally the word meant 'an oriental priest, learned in astrology'

Magnificat: the first word of Mary's song; Latin: *magnifies*; the Song begins: 'My soul magnifies the Lord'

A: Jesus: his birth

Make sure you have read and understood the set texts: Matthew 1:18–2:23; Luke 1:26–2:40.

The birth narratives in Matthew and Luke

All the New Testament writers are agreed that Jesus was the Son of God; however, there are only two Gospels, those of Matthew and Luke, which give any information on how this alleged Son of God came into the world. Their accounts are known as the birth narratives.

You will find the birth narratives in Matthew 1:18–2.23 and Luke 1:26–2.40. These narratives contain considerable differences. The table on page 8 will help you to identify some of them.

Matthew's version

Matthew focuses on Joseph. Following an un-named angel's announcement to him of Mary's miraculous pregnancy, Joseph marries Mary, and the baby Jesus is born in a 'house' (2:11) in Bethlehem.

We then learn that the first non-Jews to set eyes on him were Magi or Wise Men, who followed a star 'from the East'. This probably means from the east of the Jordan river, possibly from Babylonia or Egypt or Arabia.

We are not told how many of them there were. The tradition that there were three is based on the fact that there were three gifts. Neither are we told that they were kings. This tradition is based on such passages as Psalm 72:11, 'May all kings fall down before him'.

Matthew then records how the Wise Men duped Herod, and how Herod reacted by killing all the children in Bethlehem under two years old. Joseph is forewarned and flees with Mary and Jesus to Egypt. After Herod's death, they return to Nazareth.

Luke's version

Luke focuses on Mary. An angel named Gabriel tells her of her pregnancy. There is no mention of a marriage, but Mary, on a visit to her cousin, Elizabeth, who is also pregnant, expresses her joy in a famous hymn known as the Magnificat. Elizabeth gives birth to John the Baptist, whereupon her husband, Zechariah, makes a famous prophecy known as the Benedictus.

We are then told of a census called by Caesar Augustus, which made it necessary for Joseph and Mary, who are already engaged (2:5), to travel to Bethlehem to be registered. Because there is 'no room for them in the inn', the baby Jesus is born 'in a manger', probably in a stable or outhouse. Meanwhile, some shepherds are informed by angels of Jesus' birth, and go immediately to Bethlehem to visit him.

Dürer: The Adoration of the Magi

Eight days after the birth, Jesus is presented in the Temple in Jerusalem. He is mysteriously recognised as the Messiah by Simeon and Anna, whereupon Simeon speaks a hymn known as the Nunc Dimittis. Following the presentation in the Temple, Joseph, Mary and Jesus return to their home in Nazareth.

AO1 Activity

Prepare a 30-second news flash on how Jesus' birth is presented in Matthew and a 30-second news flash on how Jesus' birth is presented in Luke.

This practises the AO1 skill of selecting and presenting the key relevant information.

quickfire

1.1 Where do Matthew's Old Testament quotations come from?

Differences in the accounts

Matthew writes from Joseph's viewpoint, Luke from Mary's.

Matthew alone records Joseph and Mary's marriage, the appearance of the star, the visit of the Wise Men, the slaughter of the infants and the flight to Egypt.

Matthew has extensive quotations from the Old Testament. Luke does not.

Luke mentions that Jesus was born 'in a manger'. Matthew speaks of a 'house'.

Luke alone records Mary's visit to Elizabeth, the birth of John the Baptist, the visit of the shepherds, the presentation of Christ in the Temple, and the three hymns (the *Magnificat*, the *Benedictus* and the *Nunc Dimittis*).

Differences between the birth narratives in Matthew and Luke

Detail	Matthew / Luke
Angels	Un-named angel appears to Joseph (Angel quotes from Isaiah 7:14)
	Angel Gabriel appears to Mary (the **Annunciation**)
Mary and Joseph	Joseph marries Mary (1:24)
	Joseph is engaged to Mary (1:27, 2:5)
	Mary visits Elizabeth
	Mary's Song – The *Magnificat*
	The birth of John the Baptist
	Zechariah's prophecy – The *Benedictus*
	The census
Visitors	The Wise Men (Quotes from Micah 5:2 and 2 Samuel 5:2)
	The Shepherds
Herod	The slaughter of the infants
	(Quotes from Jeremiah 31:15)
Temple	The presentation of Christ in the Temple Simeon's Song – The *Nunc Dimittis*
Return journey	The flight to Egypt
	(Quotes from Hosea 11:1)
	The return to Nazareth from Egypt (Another quotation, but the exact reference is unknown. It may be a reference to Samson, see Judges 13:5,7)
	The return to Nazareth from Jerusalem
Chronology	Matthew simply states that Jesus was born 'in the days of Herod the king' (2:1).
	Luke is more specific. We are told that it was 'when Quirinius was governor of Syria' (2:2).

Key terms

Annunciation: Gabriel's announcement to Mary

Historicity: historical accuracy

The historicity of the accounts

Matthew gives little historical detail, but he does mention Herod's massacre of the children of Bethlehem. Because this massacre is not reported by any other contemporary historian, some people think that Matthew invented it in order to draw a parallel between Jesus and Moses, the Old Testament hero who was similarly threatened by Pharaoh. It accords well, however, with what we know of Herod's character. We know that he murdered three of his own sons in order to protect his power.

Luke (1:3) insists on the historical accuracy of his Gospel. His **chronology** of Jesus' birth, however, appears to be mistaken.

He writes that it happened when Quirinius was governor of Syria. We know that Quirinius governed Syria, which included Judea, from 6 CE to 12 CE, but it cannot be established that he was governor 'in the days of Herod', who died in 4 BCE. Unless he served a previous term of office, or unless some scribe miscopied Quirinius for Saturninus, who was governor from 9 BCE to 6 CE, Luke's chronology must be erroneous. Moreover, while it is true that Quirinius did indeed hold a census in 6 or 7 CE, there is no other evidence of a 'first enrolment' being held several years earlier except this statement by Luke.

Some scholars have also argued that Luke misleads his readers with regard to the three hymns that he includes in his narrative – Mary's Song (the *Magnificat*), Zechariah's prophecy (the *Benedictus*) and Simeon's Song (the *Nunc Dimittis*). These songs, they say, are hymns that were already in use by the early Christian community before Luke attributed them to various characters in his Gospel.

Study tip

Make sure that you do not confuse what Matthew says with what Luke says.

Supernatural events in the accounts

Many people doubt the historicity of the accounts because of the amazing events that they claim accompanied Jesus' birth:

- In Matthew, an angel appears to Joseph on three occasions (to announce that Mary's child is conceived of the **Holy Spirit** and to herald the beginning and end of the flight to Egypt). An angel also appears to the Wise Men, as does a star, which guides them miraculously to Jesus.

- In Luke, the angel Gabriel appears to Mary; when the pregnant Mary visits Elizabeth, Elizabeth's unborn baby leaps in her womb as he recognises the unborn Jesus. The shepherds are visited by a choir of angels. Jesus is mysteriously recognised as the Messiah by Simeon and Anna in the Temple.

The most amazing element of all is that both Matthew and Luke claim that Jesus was conceived of the Holy Spirit and born of a virgin. Thus he was human by virtue of his mother and divine by virtue of being conceived by God. His birth is a miracle. This clearly explains why there are conflicting views and models presented later in Christianity to explain how Jesus could be both human and divine.

Coreggio: The Holy Night

Key terms

Chronology: timing

Holy Spirit: God as he is active in the world

Key quote

I … decided, after investigating everything carefully from the very first, to write an orderly account. (Luke 1:3)

quickfire

1.2 Why is Luke's chronology suspect?

Key quote

Our dear friend Luke, the doctor,
and Demas send greetings.

(Colossians 4:14)

Key terms

Betrothed: engaged to be married

Redaction criticism: the theory
that New Testament writers altered
existing material about Jesus to suit
their own agenda

Harmonising the accounts

The differences between the accounts have also caused some people to doubt their veracity. If the stories were true, they argue, they would be more consistent.

However, as the accounts do not blatantly contradict one another, there is no reason why both of them cannot be true. Matthew may have had access to information that was not available to Luke, and vice versa. Some people believe that Luke may have received the story of Jesus' birth directly from Mary herself. That would explain his account of the Annunciation, the visit to Elizabeth and the presentation in the Temple. But there may have been a tradition that an angel visited Joseph as well. Also why cannot Jesus have been visited by both Wise Men and shepherds? Joseph, Mary and Jesus may have fled to Egypt sometime after Jesus was presented in the Temple.

There are also obvious similarities. Both Matthew and Luke agree that Jesus was born in Bethlehem when Herod was king of Judea, that the name of his mother was Mary, that she was **betrothed** to Joseph, that Jesus was conceived by the Holy Spirit, that Mary was a virgin and that people travelled to visit the newborn baby. They also agree that Jesus was the fulfilment of Old Testament prophecy and that he came to save not only the Jews but all humankind.

Study tip

Candidates often lose marks for incorrectly spelling key words such as 'shepherds', 'Herod', 'Gabriel', etc.

Redaction criticism

The differences that we have noted in the birth narratives may be attributed to Matthew and Luke's different theological perspectives. Many scholars believe that the Gospel writers edited pre-existing material to suit their own purposes. They not only collected material about Jesus; they also interpreted it to address a particular situation or to reach a particular audience. The study of how they did this is known as redaction criticism.

Redaction criticism had its beginnings in Germany in the late 1940s. It assumes that the original traditions about Jesus circulated as independent units in the early church. Each Gospel writer chose the material that he wanted and arranged it to suit his own theological interests, making significant additions and omissions and changing the wording in order to make a theological point.

Thus, it is argued that Matthew's Gospel was aimed at Jewish readers. He tells the story of Jesus' birth from Joseph's viewpoint. He is at pains to prove that Jesus was connected, through Joseph, with Israel's legendary King David, and that he is the fulfilment of the Old Testament revelation of God. His account contains four quotations from Old Testament prophets (Isaiah, Micah, Jeremiah and Hosea) and one each from two other Old Testament books, 2 Samuel and, possibly, the Book of Judges. He is convinced, however, that Jesus has come into the world not only for the Jews but for all peoples, and expresses that conviction by recording that his very first visitors were foreigners, Wise Men 'from the east'.

Luke, too, is convinced that Jesus has universal significance. As Simeon's Song puts it, he is 'a light to lighten the Gentiles'. But Luke's emphasis differs from that of Matthew. Luke, who was probably Paul's friend, 'Luke, the beloved physician', mentioned in Colossians 4.14, is the only non-Jewish writer in the New Testament.

Luke's Gospel, which is a prologue to his second book, the Book of Acts, appears to be aimed specifically at Gentiles, and both books are dedicated to a man with a Greek name, Theophilus. Some people believe that this name, which means 'lover of God' may be a general term for all those who follow Jesus.

Whereas Matthew's Gospel has a Jewish flavour, the flavour of Luke's is distinctly Greek. For instance, he appeals less to the Old Testament than Matthew, and when he does, he quotes not from the Hebrew but from the Greek version, the Septuagint.

Luke tells the story of Jesus' birth not from Joseph's viewpoint, but from Mary's. This may be because he is less anxious than Matthew to establish a connection between Jesus and King David. It also shows his sympathy for those, including women, who were marginalised in the society of his time. Throughout his Gospel, Luke emphasises that Jesus brought salvation to the poor and the needy, and that the grace of God is bestowed especially on the underprivileged and downtrodden.

Note that in Luke's Gospel, the good news of Jesus' birth is brought for the first time not to sophisticated Wise Men, who could afford expensive gifts, but to poor shepherds tending their flock by night. The story of the presentation of Christ in the Temple also makes clear that Joseph and Mary were poor people. The sacrifice they make is the sacrifice of the poor ('a pair of turtledoves or two young pigeons'). On such occasions, wealthy people were expected to sacrifice a lamb (see Leviticus 12.8). This story, together with the prominence given to the birth of John the Baptist, emphasises the connection between Jesus and the Jewish religion. So that, despite the Greek flavour of his Gospel, Luke, like Matthew, is convinced that Jesus is the fulfilment of the Old Testament revelation of God. John the Baptist represents the last of the Old Testament prophets, but he is no match for Jesus.

AO1 Activity

After reading the section on redaction criticism, close the book and write down the reasons that redaction criticism suggests for three key differences between Matthew's and Luke's accounts of Jesus' birth. Then compare answers with someone else and consider whether or not you want to change your own list.

Study tip

Redaction criticism should not be used simply to imply that the Gospel writers cannot be trusted. This view must be balanced with an understanding that although they were primarily concerned with theological matters, they were also writing history.

quickfire

1.3 What are the Jewish elements in Matthew's account of Jesus' birth?

Key term

Gentiles: non-Jews

quickfire

1.4 How does Luke's account of Jesus' birth reflect his sympathy for the poor?

Specification content

Interpretation and application of the birth narratives to the doctrine of the incarnation (substantial presence and the kenotic model).

The doctrine of the incarnation

The English word **incarnation** comes from the Latin word *incarnationem*, which is made up of two basic elements, *in + carnis*: flesh. Incarnation, therefore, means 'becoming flesh'.

The doctrine of the incarnation expresses the belief that Jesus Christ was God in human form. According to this belief, Jesus' life on earth was only a short period in the story of one who had always been and will always be. His birth at Bethlehem was not the beginning of this story, nor was his death on the cross at Calvary the end. The belief asserts that while Jesus lived on earth people found themselves in the presence of God in the flesh. As the Gospel according to John puts it (1:14), 'the Word became flesh and dwelt among us, full of grace and truth; we have beheld his glory, glory as of the only Son from the Father'.

The most widely accepted definitions of the incarnation and the nature of Jesus were made by the First Council of Nicea in 325, the Council of Ephesus in 431 and the Council of Chalcedon in 451. Extracts from the Nicene and Chalcedonian creeds are printed below.

What they assert is that Jesus Christ was both fully God: begotten from, but not created by the Father; and fully man: taking his flesh and human nature from the Virgin Mary.

These two natures, human and divine, were united in the one person of Jesus. This is known as 'the **hypostatic union**'.

Key quote

We believe … in one Lord Jesus Christ, the Son of God, begotten of the Father (the only-begotten; that is, of the essence of the Father), God of God, Light of Light, very God of very God, begotten not made, being of one substance with the Father … who for us men and for our salvation came down from heaven and was incarnate and was made man.
(First Council of Nicea 325)

Key terms

Hypostatic union: the combination of the divine and human nature in the Person of Christ

Incarnation: God becoming flesh in Jesus

Extracts from the Nicene and Chalcedonian creeds

It is most important to understand that the doctrine of the incarnation does not see Jesus as half human, half God. Rather, it states that Jesus is fully God and fully human.

- He is fully God because he is believed to have existed from the beginning with God, and was God. His appearance here on earth was only a brief period in this existence. After his resurrection, he is believed to have returned to his Father, with whom he now reigns for evermore.

- He is fully human because he was a man of flesh and blood, born as any other person is born; he was a helpless baby; he had to learn to walk and talk, like every other child (Luke 2:40, 52); he ate and slept and drank; he experienced hunger, weakness, temptation and disappointment; he died, like all human beings do.

Study tip

A common mistake is to say that the doctrine of the incarnation asserts that Jesus was half God, half-human. It does not. It asserts that Jesus was *fully* God and *fully* human.

The Person of Jesus, therefore, combines two natures – a divine nature and human nature. The doctrine of the incarnation gives equal validity to both.

The theory is rejected by Jews and Muslims, and some Christian denominations such as Unitarians, on the grounds that it violates the transcendence and immutability of God. Nevertheless, Christian theologians throughout the ages who have attemped to emphasise one nature in Jesus' Person at the expense of the other have been condemned by the church as heretics.

AO1 Activity

Design a simple flow-chart to explain the doctrine of the incarnation and to show that you have a personal understanding or 'ownership' of the concept.

Incarnation as kenosis

The term **kenosis** comes from the Greek verb *kenó*, to make empty. It appears in Paul's Letter to the Philippians (2:7), where Paul says that Jesus, 'though he was in the form of God, did not regard equality with God as something to be exploited, but **emptied** himself, taking the form of a slave, being born in human likeness'.

Kenotic theology attempts to understand the incarnation in this light. Its main concern is to solve some of the difficulties arising from Jesus having both a divine nature and a human nature; for example, how could an omniscient God become a baby, and how could Jesus, if he was God, be tempted (Mark 1:13) or not know when the world was to end (Mark 13:32)?

The basic question is what does Paul mean when he says that Christ 'emptied' himself? It cannot be that Jesus emptied himself of his divinity and ceased to be God, for if he was truly God, he must have continued to be God during his earthly ministry, maintaining the **substantial presence** of God, although his divine attributes were hidden.

The 'emptying' consists of:

- A **preincarnate** self-limitation by Jesus – agreeing to take 'the form of a slave, being born in human likeness' and hence fully human whilst maintaining substantial presence as fully divine.

- The self-emptying of his own will as a human being and submitting entirely to the will of God.

- The kenotic theory is an indication of God's will and of Jesus' ethic of sacrifice.

Key quote

We … confess one and the same Son, our Lord Jesus Christ, the same perfect in Godhead and also perfect in manhood; truly God and truly man … consubstantial with the Father according to the Godhead, and consubstantial with us according to the Manhood; in all things like us, without sin; begotten before all ages of the Father according to the Godhead, and in these latter days, for us and for our salvation, born of the Virgin Mary, the Mother of God, according to the Manhood; one and the same Christ, Son, Lord, only begotten, to be acknowledged in two natures … (Council of Chalcedon 451)

Key terms

Kenosis: Jesus 'emptying' himself

Preincarnate: before the incarnation

Substantial presence: the idea that, although unseen, God is fully present not symbolically but in reality or substance (as in the Eucharist for the Roman Catholic Church)

Key skills

Knowledge involves:

Selection of a range of (thorough) accurate and relevant information that is directly related to the specific demands of the question.

This means you choose the correct information relevant to the question set NOT the topic area. You will have to think and focus on selecting key information and NOT writing everything you know about the topic area.

Understanding involves:

Explanation that is extensive, demonstrating depth and/or breadth with excellent use of evidence and examples including (where appropriate) thorough and accurate supporting use of sacred texts, sources of wisdom and specialist language.

This means that you demonstrate that you understand something by being able to illustrate and expand your points through examples/supporting evidence in a personal way and NOT repeat chunks from a text book (known as rote learning).

Further application of skills:

Go through the topic areas in this section and create some bullet lists of key points from key areas. For each one, provide further elaboration and explanation through the use of evidence and examples.

AO1 Developing skills

It is now time to reflect upon the information that has been covered so far. It is also important to consider how what you have learned can be focused and used for examination-style answers by practising the skills associated with AO1.

Assessment objective 1 (AO1) involves demonstrating knowledge and understanding. The terms 'knowledge' and 'understanding' are obvious but it is crucial to be familiar with how certain skills demonstrate these terms, and also, how the performance of these skills is measured (see generic band descriptors Band 5 for AS AO1).

Obviously, an answer is placed within an appropriate band descriptor depending upon how well the answer performs, ranging from excellent, good, satisfactory, basic/limited to very limited.

To begin with, try using the framework / writing frame provided to help you in practising these skills to answer the question below.

As the units in each section of the book develop, the amount of support will be reduced gradually in order to encourage your independence and the perfecting of your AO1 skills.

EXAM PRACTICE: A WRITING FRAME

Examine the differences between Matthew's and Luke's accounts of Jesus' birth.

The accounts of Jesus' birth in Matthew and Luke are known as …

Matthew focuses on …

Luke focuses on …

There are several examples of differences in their accounts. They include …

Luke's chronology is particularly suspect because …

It is not, however, impossible to harmonise the accounts by suggesting …

Redaction critics argue that the differences in the accounts may be attributed to …

In conclusion …

Issues for analysis and evaluation

The extent to which the birth narratives provide insight into the doctrine of the incarnation

This section covers AO2 content and skills

Specification content
The extent to which the birth narratives provide insight into the doctrine of the incarnation.

The insight can be measured by either accepting or rejecting the accounts of Jesus' birth given by Matthew and Luke, especially with regard to the alleged virgin birth.

There are those who reject the concept of the virgin birth on the following grounds:

Matthew's account sees the birth of Jesus as the fulfilment of the prophecy in Isaiah 7:14. Matthew states that 'All this took place to fulfill what had been spoken by the Lord through the prophet: "Look, the virgin shall conceive and bear a son ..."'

Matthew is quoting from the Septuagint, where the Greek uses the word *Parthenos* = virgin to translate the Hebrew word *'almah*. The word *'almah*, however, does not technically mean 'a virgin', but rather 'a young woman of marriageable age'. Thus, Isaiah did not necessarily expect the Messiah to be born of a virgin. Many believe that the text refers to the nation of Israel giving birth to a Messiah.

There are several instances in ancient mythology of heroes being born of a virgin, e.g. Hercules, who was the son of a divine father and a human mother. The virgin birth story could therefore have been made up by the early Christian church, which wanted to portray Jesus as the Son of God.

The story corresponds well to other supernatural elements associated with the account of Jesus' birth in both Matthew and Luke, for example angelic visitations, and in Matthew the appearance of a mysterious star. The alleged appearance of a star was a common occurrence at the birth of a notable person in the ancient world.

All these things, it is claimed, belong to the realm of mythology, and the birth narratives would be more credible without them.

Accordingly, some scholars, led by the German scholar, Rudolf, Bultmann, have called for the birth narratives, too, to be demythologised.

There are others who readily accept the virgin birth accounts. They argue that early Christian writers were unlikely to be influenced by pagan myths.

It is also significant that despite the differences between them, both Matthew and Luke agree on the essential points about Jesus' birth: that he was conceived by the Holy Spirit and that Mary was a virgin.

Luke insists on the historical accuracy of his Gospel. Paul, too, in several of his Letters, provides testimony that Christians believed from the earliest times that Jesus was the Son of God.

What is important in the story is the entry of God into his creation – the incarnation. If this miracle is accepted, then the virgin birth presents no difficulty. If it is accepted that Jesus is God, it is natural to believe that he entered the world in a supernatural way.

In conclusion, despite the debate about accepting or rejecting the miracle of the incarnation through the virgin birth, what could be argued is that insight into the doctrine of the incarnation does not depend upon the historicity of this event. The issue of insight into the doctrine of the incarnation may be more dependent on the specific interpretation of, and the understanding that follows for, the believer, about the nature of Jesus' birth. This, then, could surely be matter of faith?

AO2 Activity *Possible lines of argument*

Listed below are some conclusions that could be drawn from the AO2 reasoning in the above text:

1. The birth narratives in Matthew and Luke are credible historical accounts.
2. The birth narratives in Matthew and Luke are myths.
3. The birth narratives in Matthew and Luke were made up by the early church.

Consider each of the conclusions drawn above and collect evidence and examples to support each argument from the AO1 and AO2 material studied in this section. Select one conclusion that you think is most convincing and explain why it is so. Now contrast this with the weakest conclusion in the list, justifying your argument with clear reasoning and evidence.

Specification content

The relative importance of redaction criticism for understanding the biblical birth narratives.

The relative importance of redaction criticism for understanding the biblical birth narratives

Redaction criticism is the theory that New Testament writers altered existing material about Jesus to suit their own agenda. It assumes that the original traditions about Jesus circulated as independent units in the early church. Each Gospel writer chose the material that he wanted and arranged it to suit his own theological interests, making significant additions and omissions and changing the wording in order to make a theological point.

In favour of redaction criticism, it may be said that it treats the Gospel writers as individual authors with a particular agenda, not as impersonal transcribers of existing material.

It allows us to understand the author's purpose, e.g. that Matthew is writing for Jews and Luke for Gentiles, and can shed light on the *Sitz im Leben* (a German term meaning 'life setting') of the communities for which the Gospels were written, e.g. that Matthew's audience needed more proof from the Hebrew scriptures than did that of Luke.

It shows that the Gospels are not primarily concerned with chronological accounts of historic events, but have theological agendas. They must be read primarily as theology, not history. However, redaction criticism has been criticised for not being based on sufficient evidence. For instance, it cannot be conclusively proved that the Gospel writers used pre-existing material, and even if they did, we cannot assume that they would feel free to adapt it. Moreover, it is not clear that the early church would be able to recognise the author's specific theological points. There is therefore a danger that the theory may lead to the reconstruction of a *Sitz im Leben* without sufficient evidence.

Redaction criticism is nevertheless a useful reminder that the Gospel writers were writing theology, not history and that they had a variety of potential audiences.

In conclusion, one possible solution could be that there are some advantages to redaction criticism in that it can give insight into theological perspectives held by the authors and in this sense is an interesting pursuit. How serious the results of such intellectual pursuits are, is directly challenged by several factors:

Firstly, the result depends upon the accuracy of the redactor, whether the original Gospel writer but more specifically the scholar identifying the possible redaction, and then extracting the complete redaction in its entirety. For example, has every relevant part of the original narrative been removed and equally, is every aspect that has been removed relevant?

Secondly, redaction criticism in no way informs historical analysis and is of more value in theological terms. The real danger in this is for Christianity as a whole and the interpretation of the Bible, and each of the books therein, as containing a single coherent theology and history, or a selection of varied theologies and variants of historical events.

Finally, as with anything, the objectivity of the redactor needs to be established if the result is beyond a simple procedure of finding other than that which they were initially looking for!

AO2 Activity Possible lines of argument

Listed below are some conclusions that could be drawn from the AO2 reasoning in the above text:

1. Redaction criticism is critical for understanding the birth narratives.

2. Redaction criticism is of some use for understanding the birth narratives.

3. Redaction criticism is worthless for understanding the birth narratives.

Consider each of the conclusions drawn above and collect evidence and examples to support each argument from the AO1 and AO2 material studied in this section. Select one conclusion that you think is most convincing and explain why it is so. Now contrast this with the weakest conclusion in the list, justifying your argument with clear reasoning and evidence.

AO2 Developing skills

It is now time to reflect upon the information that has been covered so far. It is also important to consider how what you have learned can be focused and used for examination-style answers by practising the skills associated with AO2.

Assessment objective 2 (AO2) involves 'analysis' and 'evaluation'. The terms may be obvious but it is crucial to be familiar with how certain skills demonstrate these terms, and also, how the performance of these skills is measured (see generic band descriptors Band 5 for AS AO2).

Obviously, an answer is placed within an appropriate band descriptor depending upon how well the answer performs, ranging from excellent, good, satisfactory, basic/limited to very limited.

For starters, try using the framework / writing frame provided to help you in practising these skills to answer the question below.

As the units in each section of the book develop, the amount of support will be reduced gradually in order to encourage your independence and the perfecting of your AO2 skills.

Have a go at answering this question by using the writing frame below.

EXAM PRACTICE: A WRITING FRAME

To claim that Jesus was both God and man makes no sense at all.

The issue for debate here is the reasonableness or otherwise of the doctrine of the incarnation, which asserts that …

The contention would be accepted by Jews and Muslims, and some Christian denominations such as Unitarians, on the grounds that …

It would, however, be rejected by most mainstream Christian traditions on the grounds that …

It is my view that … and I base this argument on the following reasons:

Key skills

Analysis involves identifying issues raised by the materials in the AO1, together with those identified in the AO2 section, and presents sustained and clear views, either of scholars or from a personal perspective ready for evaluation.

This means that it picks out key things to debate and the lines of argument presented by others or a personal point of view.

Evaluation involves considering the various implications of the issues raised based upon the evidence gleaned from analysis and provides an extensive detailed argument with a clear conclusion.

This means that the answer weighs up the various and different lines of argument analysed through individual commentary and response and arrives at a conclusion through a clear process of reasoning.

This section covers AO1 content and skills

Specification content

Interpretation and application to the understanding of death, the soul, the resurrected body and the afterlife, with reference to Matthew 10:28; John 20–21; 1 Corinthians 15; Philippians 1:21–24.

Key terms

Chiasm: a style of writing that repeats similar ideas in reverse sequence (ABCBA)

Messiah: the saviour of the Jews promised in the Old Testament

Resurrection: rising from the dead

Key person

John: author of the fourth Gospel

quickfire

1.5   What is a chiasm?

B: Jesus: his resurrection

Make sure you have read and understood the set texts: Matthew 10:28; John 20–21; 1 Corinthians 15; Philippians 1:21–24.

The English word resurrection comes from the Latin *resurrectio*, which means 'to rise again'. Christians believe that, following his death on the cross and his burial, Jesus rose again from the dead, and for a period of forty days appeared to many of his followers. The Gospels of Matthew, Mark and Luke record that he warned his disciples 'that he must go to Jerusalem and suffer many things from the elders and chief priests and scribes, and be killed, and on the third day be raised'. At the time, his words had little effect on the disciples. When Jesus was arrested, they were thrown into utter confusion and fled. Yet, within a short time of his crucifixion, they had become convinced that he was still alive. They began to preach that God had raised him from the dead, thus proving that he was the Messiah, and that, by accepting his messiahship, people could share in his resurrection. This was a great comfort to them as they embarked on their Christian mission. Jesus had already warned them that they faced persecution, but that they need not fear those who can only 'kill the body' (Matthew 10:28).

The resurrection in John 20–21

John 20

Commentators have drawn attention to the highly structured nature of John's resurrection account. In chapter 20 we have a series of five episodes in which the risen Jesus overcomes the disciples' sorrow, fear and doubt to bring them to faith:

- John, the beloved disciple, 'saw and believed' (20:8).
- Mary comes to believe when she hears Jesus call her name (20:16).
- The disciples recognise Jesus, and receive the Holy Spirit (20:22).
- Thomas believes when he is allowed to touch Jesus' wounds (20:28).
- John says that those who read this evidence will believe (20:31).

The five episodes form what is known as a chiasm. A chiasm is a style of writing that repeats similar ideas in reverse sequence (ABCBA). In the first and last, the risen Jesus does not appear, but people come to believe in the resurrection on the basis of evidence (the linen wrappings in 20:8, the testimony of others in 20:31). In the second and fourth episodes, Jesus appears to individuals who fail to recognise him. At the centre of the chiasm, he imparts the Holy Spirit to the disciples.

When the disciple 'whom Jesus loved' (20:2) entered the tomb, 'he saw and believed' (20:8). We are told in the next verse, however, that he and Peter as yet did not understand the scripture, that Jesus must rise from the dead. John sees an empty tomb and the linen wrappings rolled up and realises that something strange has happened. But neither he nor Peter understand the meaning of what they see. They can testify to Jesus' empty tomb, but not yet to his resurrection.

John 13:23 identifies the disciple 'whom Jesus loved' as John.

When Jesus appears to Mary Magdalene, she does not recognise him at first and supposes him to be the gardener. This is typical of other encounters with the risen Jesus (there is a similar example in John 21:4, where his disciples fail to recognise him when he appears by the Sea of Galilee), and suggests that there had been some change in his resurrection body.

Jesus then sends Mary with a message for the disciples. She, a woman, becomes 'an apostle to the apostles'. 'Go to my brothers,' Jesus tells her, 'and say to them, "I am ascending to my Father and your Father, to my God and your God".' His returning to the Father is good news for the disciples, for they know that he has promised to send them the Holy Spirit, who will teach them all things (John 14:16–17). They are also brought into a new and intimate relationship that unites them as brothers with Jesus sharing the fatherhood of God.

On the evening of the day of the resurrection, Jesus appears to the disciples as a group (20:19–23). Again, it appears that his body has undergone some change, for he is able to move through locked doors and the disciples do not seem to recognise him until he shows them the wounds in his hands and his side.

Jesus immediately commissions the disciples (20:21): 'As the Father has sent me, so I send you'. These words have implications for the mission of the church. The church is not a human institution. It is commissioned by Jesus, the risen Son of God.

We are then told that Jesus breathed on the disciples and said to them, 'Receive the Holy Spirit'. The verb 'breathed on' is the same as that used in Genesis 2:7 to describe God's action when he created man from the dust of the ground and 'breathed into his nostrils the breath of life'. It implies that there is here the beginning of a new creation, the Christian Church.

The giving of the Spirit in 20:22 raises the question of whether John is describing the same event as that described by Luke in Acts 2:1–13, the Holy Spirit descending on the apostles on the day of Pentecost.

The evidence suggests that there were two different events. The giving of the Spirit in John does not seem to have inspired the disciples: a week later they are back in the room with locked doors (20:26); in the next chapter they are fishing. Moreover, Jesus' promise was that the Spirit would be given only after he had returned to the Father (see John 16:7), and that has not yet happened. Thus, the giving of the Spirit in John seems to mark the inauguration of the church's mission. The mission does not actually begin until the outpouring of the Spirit on Pentecost.

Jesus then develops his commission. He is returning to the Father, but is sending the disciples to proclaim his good news to all the world. Only God (and Jesus, being God) can forgive sins, but now that God lives in the disciples in the person of the Holy Spirit, the power is extended to them as well. They are commissioned to carry on God's work. The world will be forced to choose for or against Jesus. Those who believe will have their sins forgiven; those who refuse will be condemned.

Study tip

Stronger candidates often make reference to a similar account of the appearance to the disciples and of the commission in Luke 24:36–49.

Key term

Apostle (from Greek apóstolos): 'one who is sent'), messenger, ambassador; the name given to those sent by Jesus to proclaim his good news

Key quote

On the evening of that first day of the week, when the disciples were together, with the doors locked for fear of the Jewish leaders, Jesus came and stood among them and said, 'Peace be with you!' After he said this, he showed them his hands and side. The disciples were overjoyed when they saw the Lord. (John 20:19–20)

quickfire

1.6 What does the giving of the Spirit in John 20:22 signify?

Caravaggio: Doubting Thomas

John now records that Thomas had not been present when Jesus first appeared to the disciples. When they tell him that they have seen the Lord, he does not believe them. A week later, they are again in a locked room, and Thomas is with them (20:26). When Jesus appears, he challenges Thomas to believe (20:27), and invites him, in words that suggest that he is aware of his request (20:25), to feel his wounds. Thomas' confession (20:28) is a climax to the chapter.

The chapter ends with John's statement that his purpose in writing his Gospel is to enable people to believe without having seen, and thus to experience the blessedness that comes through faith.

John 21

Chapter 21 can be divided into three sections:

(a) Jesus appears to the disciples by the Sea of Galilee (1–14)

Jesus is described as standing on the shore. There is no explanation of how he got there. Equally mysterious is how he knows that there is an abundant catch of fish on the right side of the disciples' boat (21:6) and where he got the bread and fish that are already prepared on the charcoal fire (21:9).

(b) Jesus commissions Peter to shepherd his people (21:15–23)

After breakfast Jesus asks Peter, whom he addresses by his former name, Simon, son of John, whether he loves him 'more than these', probably referring to the other disciples. When Simon replies that he does, Jesus commands him: 'Feed my lambs'. However, Jesus asks the same question twice again, and receives two similar commands: 'Tend my sheep' and 'Feed my sheep'. The three commands taken together form a comprehensive image of shepherding, which was a familiar way of describing God's care for his people.

After Peter professes his love, Jesus spells out the cost of that love. John tells us that Jesus' words in 21:18 describe the kind of death by which Peter would glorify God. There is a tradition that Peter was crucified head down during Nero's persecution of the church in AD 67. However, some scholars have pointed out that these may not be true words of Jesus. As John's Gospel was not written until late in the 1st Century CE, the author would already know how Peter had died.

(c) John's testimony confirmed

John 21:24 identifies the author of the Gospel as John, the Beloved Disciple. This does not necessarily mean that John actually did the writing. The writing may have been done by his disciples. But it does mean that John was responsible for what was written. His Gospel claims to be an eyewitness account. His disciples assert that they know that John's testimony is true. This may mean either that some of the disciples too had been eyewitnesses to the resurrection appearances or that the Holy Spirit has confirmed John's testimony to them.

The Gospel ends with one last testimony to the inexhaustible greatness of Jesus. It is not clear whether it is the testimony of John himself, or of one of his disciples, or of some later scribe who added his own comment to the text.

quickfire

1.7 What were the risen Jesus' three commands to Peter?

Key quote

This is the disciple who is testifying to these things and has written them, and we know that his testimony is true. **(John 21:24)**

Conrad Witz: The Miraculous Draught of Fishes

Paul's understanding of the resurrection: 1 Corinthians 15

In Philippians 1:21–24 Paul tells us that because of the resurrection 'dying is gain' and he longs 'to be with Christ' and some argue that it suggests that at death we are immediately, in some sense, with Christ.

In his treatise on the resurrection in 1 Corinthians 15, Paul accepts without question that the resurrection of Jesus was an objective fact. He does so on the basis of his own experience. In Acts 9:1–20 we read how the risen Jesus appeared to Paul as he journeyed from Jerusalem to Damascus to persecute Christians in that city, and how Paul then came to be a Christian himself. He recounts this experience in I Corinthians 15:5–9. The risen Jesus, he writes, had appeared 'to more than five hundred brethren at one time … Last of all … he appeared also to me … the least of the apostles, unfit to be called an apostle, because I persecuted the church of God'.

He goes on to argue (15:12–19) that Christian believers too are resurrected. The proof of their resurrection lies in Jesus' own resurrection. If there is no resurrection, then Jesus himself was not resurrected. And if Jesus was not resurrected, the Christian faith is not only futile, because those who have died 'have perished', but untruthful as well, because it is founded on a lie. The fact is, he asserts, that Jesus has been raised. He refers to the Fall of Adam in Genesis 3. By his disobedience to God the first man, Adam, had brought death into the world. By his total obedience to God the perfect man, Jesus, has brought resurrection. But there is a specific order. Christ, 'the first fruits', has already been resurrected. 'Those who belong to Christ', Christian believers, will be resurrected 'at his coming' at the end of time to judge the world, when 'the trumpet will sound, and the dead will be raised imperishable' (15:52).

In 15:35–50 he discusses the question: with what kind of body are the dead raised? He uses the analogy of seed planting. The body that is 'planted' in the earth is perishable, dishonourable, weak, physical. The body that is raised is imperishable, glorious, strong, spiritual. The resurrection body, therefore, so excels over the earthly body as a fully grown plant excels over its seed. 'The man of heaven' excels over 'the man of dust'. Thus, it is obvious that, for Paul, as for Jesus in his teaching on the resurrection in Luke 20:36, the resurrection body is a new and different body.

Resurrection, therefore, is not the same as resuscitation. When Jesus raised to life Jairus' daughter and the widow's son at Nain and Lazarus, he resuscitated them. They returned from the dead exactly as they were when they were alive. His own resurrection, however, was different. His resurrected body was not the same as his earthly body. He appeared 'in another form' (Mark 16:12). Mary Magdalene failed to recognise him (John 20:14), as did the disciples on the Emmaus Road (Luke 24:16). He could now walk through locked doors (John 20:19) and vanish from sight (Luke 24:31). The body of the risen Christ is a new mode of existence, and the resurrection body of Christians will be in the image of this (I Corinthians 15:49).

Paul does not, however, give any indication of how this change will be effected. Neither does he say if it happens at the death of each individual or to all collectively at some future time. Nor is there any clear teaching on whether it happens to all and sundry or only to believers. He is simply telling the Corinthians, many of whom undoubtedly believed in the Greek idea that only the soul was immortal, that there will be a resurrection not only of the soul but of the body as well, but that the resurrection body will not operate according to the laws of the flesh but according to the laws of the spirit.

Key person

Paul: a 1st-century apostle who preached Christianity mostly to Gentiles

Key quote

But God gives it a body as he has determined, and to each kind of seed he gives its own body. Not all flesh is the same: people have one kind of flesh, animals have another, birds another and fish another. There are also heavenly bodies and there are earthly bodies; but the splendour of the heavenly bodies is one kind, and the splendour of the earthly bodies is another.
(1 Corinthians 15:38–40)

quickfire

1.8 What is the difference between *resuscitation* and *resurrection*?

Study tip

Make sure you have understood Paul's argument in 1 Corinthians 15, and can comment on it.

Modern interpretation: Rudolf Bultmann and N. T. Wright

Rudolf Bultmann

Rudolf Bultmann (1884–1976) was a German theologian who argued that all that is necessary for Christian belief is that Jesus lived, preached and died by crucifixion. He was convinced of the need to **demythologise** the New Testament, to interpret it in terms that modern readers can understand.

- Bultmann defines 'myth' as 'the report of an event or occurrence in which supernatural, superhuman powers or persons are at work'.

- It is a way in which people attempt:
  (i) to explain the world in which they live and their existence in it;
  (ii) to explain the divine in human terms.

- An example is the ancient belief in a 'three-tiered universe', where the earth was a sphere, with Heaven above and Hell beneath.

- Jesus' virgin birth and resurrection are classified as myths.

- Since New Testament use the mythological terminology of their time, it is impossible for modern readers to believe their accounts without discarding all modern intellect and knowledge.

- Bultmann therefore attempts to interpret the New Testament in such a way that changes its 'mythological' flavour but retains its meaning.

The resurrection, Bultmann argues, was not a historical event. It is a myth, a story designed to sustain faith. He accepts that the earliest disciples believed that it was true. Paul in I Corinthians 15 even tried to prove it. One cannot, however, expect scientifically minded modern readers to believe in the resurrection of a corpse.

Bultmann's position may be summarised as follows:

- Jesus is the Son of God, not in a literal sense, but in the sense that he is the expression of God. What God had to say he initiated in Jesus.

- Belief in the resurrection of Christ's physical body is unnecessary to Christian faith. In fact, it is contrary to faith. Bultmann writes 'If the resurrection were an historical fact, faith would become superfluous. What is decisive is not that Jesus came to life again but that he is, for you, the Risen One. The one who was crucified is alive again if you see him as such with the eyes of faith.'

- Modern Christians cannot accept the resurrection with integrity because:
  (i) it can never be proved;
  (ii) even if it could be proved it could not in itself give meaning to the event of the crucifixion.

- The resurrection, in its demythologised form, is seen as the realisation that the cross of Christ was not a defeat but a victory. The disciples suddenly realised that when he suffered death, Jesus was already the Son of God. Therefore, his death by itself was a victory over the power of death. The Lord of Life had given himself over to death and had thereby conquered it.

- Thus, the crucifixion of Jesus contained the resurrection within it. There was no second historical event.

- The victory comes through the cross. Faith in the resurrection is really the same thing as faith in the saving efficacy of the cross.

- Faith in the saving efficacy of the cross comes through faith 'in the word of preaching'.

- The preaching originates from that rise of belief in the disciples.

- Easter is thus about the arising, not of Jesus, but of the faith of the early church.

Specification content

The views of R. Bultmann and N.T. Wright on the relation of the resurrection event to history and the strengths and weaknesses of these approaches.

Key term

Demythologise: to eliminate mythical elements from a piece of writing

Key person

Rudolf Bultmann: a German theologian who called for the 'demythologisation' of the New Testament

quickfire

1.9 What does the verb *to demythologise* mean?

Rudolf Bultmann

quickfire

1.10 How does Bultmann interpret the resurrection?

Key person

N. T. Wright (born 1948): a leading English New Testament scholar and former Bishop of Durham

N.T. Wright

- People receive illumination through preaching, not through any historical resurrection event.
- The resurrection takes place within individuals as they hear the word of preaching and experience the rise of faith.

Study tip

Make sure you have understood Bultmann's argument and can comment on it.

N. T. Wright

In his 817-page book, *The Resurrection of the Son of God* (2003), the English theologian N. T. Wright argues that Jesus' resurrection marks the beginning of a restoration of creation that he will complete upon his return. The following is a summary.

1. Greek and Jewish belief about life after death and resurrection

i. *Greek thought*

- There is no evidence in Greek philosophy of any belief in bodily resurrection.
- For the poet Homer, Hades, the abode of the dead, is a place of shadows.
- The philosopher Plato holds out the possibility of an afterlife for the soul, but not a bodily return to the present world.
- In a play by Euripides, Hercules rescues Alcestis from the god of death, but the play deals with mythology.

ii. *Judaism*

- In the Old Testament, the belief in resurrection is 'vague and unfocused'.
- The Hebrew Sheol, the place of the dead, is similar to Homer's Hades. People are asleep there; to wake them up is dangerous, and forbidden.
- Some Psalms (e.g. Psalm 73) express a post-mortem hope, based on God's love in the present, which will, the psalmist supposes, continue into the future.
- In Isaiah 26 and Ezekiel 37 resurrection is part of the hope for the whole nation; it will happen to all God's people at the same time.
- Daniel 12 can be interpreted in terms of an astral resurrection.
- Hosea 6 may be the earliest statement of a belief in bodily resurrection.
- In general, and unlike Platonists, who spoke of immortality only for the soul, Israelites believed in a physical resurrection, but did not agree as to whether the resurrected body would be like the former body or different in some way.
- In post-biblical Judaism, people do not pass directly from death to resurrection, but go through an interim period, after which the death of the body will be reversed. Thus, resurrection refers to the undoing of death.
- The spectrum of Jewish belief runs from the Sadducees, who deny the resurrection, to the Pharisees, who insist upon it, to Philo of Alexandria's Platonic belief in the disembodied immortality of the soul.
- Some of those who believed in the resurrection also believed in the coming of the Messiah, who would defeat God's enemies and establish God's rule.
- Some biblical texts, such as Isaiah 26, Ezekiel 37 and Daniel 12, speak of bodily resurrection, and that this was taken up by books like 2 Maccabees, by much popular thought at the time of Jesus, and by the Rabbis in the centuries after Jesus. In correspondence with the author, N T Wright has stated, 'It is vital to help people understand that 'resurrection' does not mean 'life after death' but 'life AFTER "life after death"' – that is, a newly embodied life after a period of being bodily dead.'

It was from this background that the early Christians emerged, saying two things:

- Jesus was and is the Messiah.
- This is proved because he has been raised from the dead.

Study tip

Make sure you have understood and can comment on the Jewish background to the Christian belief in resurrection.

2. Early Christian belief about life after death and resurrection

- Early Christian views about life after death belong within the Jewish spectrum, not the Greek one, but were also different.
- For almost all early Christians their ultimate hope was the resurrection of the body. There is no disagreement such as in Judaism. Some in Corinth denied the future resurrection (1 Corinthians 15:12), but Paul put them straight. Two people in 2 Timothy 2:18 say the resurrection has already happened, but they stand out by their oddity.
- In early Christianity, belief in resurrection is much more sharply focused than in Judaism. Resurrection will be an act of new creation. It will not be a simple return to the same sort of body as before; nor will it be a disembodied bliss. It will involve the gift of a new body with different properties.
- This new identity is at present kept safe by God in heaven. At the moment of resurrection it will be brought from heaven to earth. Renewed bodies need a renewed earth.
- Early Christian belief splits the resurrection into two. For Paul, it takes place in two phases: first the Messiah, then at his coming all his people.
- As those Jews who believed in resurrection spoke about the interim state of those who had died, the early Christians spoke of people being 'asleep in Christ' (e.g. 1 Corinthians 15:18).

3. The reason for early Christian belief, and the meaning of Jesus' resurrection

The early Christians believed that Jesus was the Messiah. Why? Jesus had not done what the Messiah was supposed to do. He had not won a decisive victory over Israel's enemies, nor restored the Temple, nor established God's reign in the world.

There had been other failed Messiahs – Judas the Galilean in 6 CE, Simon bar-Giora in 70 CE, bar-Kochbar in 135, but the first task of those who tried to carry on their work after their death was to find another Messiah. Why did the early Christians continue to regard Jesus as the Messiah?

- The answer that the early Christians themselves gave to this question is that Jesus was bodily raised from the dead on the third day after his crucifixion. It was his resurrection that constituted him as Messiah.
- Other Jews had died promising resurrection (cf. 2 Maccabees 7, etc.). Their followers believed that they *would* be raised from the dead; but nobody said they *had* been, for the obvious reason that they hadn't.
- It is clear that the Gospel accounts of the resurrection are about an event which happened at some interval after Jesus' death.

Key quote

But if it is preached that Christ has been raised from the dead, how can some of you say that there is no resurrection of the dead? If there is no resurrection of the dead, then not even Christ has been raised. And if Christ has not been raised, our preaching is useless and so is your faith. (1 Corinthians 15:12–14)

Key quote

The last enemy to be destroyed is death. For he 'has put everything under his feet'. (1 Corinthians 15:26–27)

quickfire

1.11 How does the early Christian belief in resurrection differ from that of the Jews?

quickfire

1.12 Why did the early Christians believe that Jesus was the Messiah?

- It is not simply a way of talking about him 'going to Heaven when he died'. Jesus was not 'resurrected to heaven'. It was forty days after the resurrection that he was exalted to heaven.
- In the Gospel narratives we find that Jesus' body is not merely a 'spiritual' presence, nor merely resuscitated, but *transformed*.
- In John's Gospel, Jesus invites the disciples to touch him to make sure he is a real human being. At the same time, he appears and disappears, sometimes through locked doors. John is telling, with bewilderment, stories about how Jesus' body was now significantly different, with new properties.

4. Conclusion

Theories that reject the resurrection may be countered as follows:

(i) *Jesus somehow survived the crucifixion.*

This can be discounted. Roman soldiers knew how to kill people.

(ii) *The tomb was empty, but nothing else happened.*

Faced with an empty tomb, and no other evidence, the disciples would have assumed that Jesus' body had been stolen, not that he had been resurrected.

(iii) *The disciples simply had visions of Jesus.*

Visions of someone recently dead are well known, but do not cause people to claim that the departed person has been raised from the dead.

- We must therefore conclude that the tomb previously housing a dead Jesus was empty, and that his followers met someone they were convinced was this same Jesus, bodily alive though in a new, transformed fashion.
- We know what conclusion the disciples drew, but they were cautious. Thomas waited before believing (John 20:26). In Matthew 28:17, some doubted.
- All other historical explanations for the origins of Christianity are less convincing than that Jesus really did rise from the dead.
- This is why the early Christians declared him to be the 'Son of God'.

Key quote

The best *historical* explanation is the one which inevitably raises all kinds of *theological* questions: the tomb was indeed empty, and Jesus was indeed seen alive, because he was truly raised from the dead.
(N. T. Wright)

AO1 Activity

Prepare a brief courtroom case to defend the claim that Jesus arose from the dead.

This will help in selecting the key, relevant information for an answer to a question on the veracity of the resurrection.

AO1 Developing skills

It is now time to reflect upon the information that has been covered so far. It is also important to consider how what you have learned can be focused and used for examination-style answers by practising the skills associated with AO1.

Assessment objective 1 (AO1) involves demonstrating knowledge and understanding. The terms 'knowledge' and 'understanding' are obvious but it is crucial to be familiar with how certain skills demonstrate these terms, and also, how the performance of these skills is measured (see generic band descriptors Band 5 for AS AO1).

▶ **Your new task is this:** from the list of ten key points below, choose six that you feel are the most important in answering the question above the list. Put your points in order of priority explaining why they are the six most important aspects to mention from that topic. This skill of prioritising and selecting appropriate material will help you in answering examination questions for AO1.

Outline N.T. Wright's argument in support of the truth of Jesus' resurrection.

1. There is no evidence in Greek thought of any belief in resurrection.

2. Jewish thought on the subject was confused. There was a belief that some Jewish heroes would be raised from the dead, but nobody thought that they had, for the rather obvious reason that they had not.

3. It was from this background that the early Christians emerged, saying that Jesus was the Messiah. The proof is that he has been raised from the dead.

4. It is clear that the Gospel accounts of the resurrection are about an event that happened at some interval after Jesus' death.

5. It is not simply a flowery way of talking about him 'going to Heaven when he died'. Jesus was not 'resurrected to heaven'. It was forty days after the resurrection that he was exalted to heaven.

6. In the Gospel narratives we find that Jesus' body is not merely a 'spiritual' presence, nor merely resuscitated, but *transformed*.

7. In John's Gospel, Jesus invites the disciples to touch him to make sure he is a real human being. But at the same time, he appears and disappears, sometimes through locked doors. John is telling, with bewilderment, stories about how Jesus' body was now significantly different, with new properties.

8. In early Christianity, belief in resurrection is much more sharply focused than in Judaism. Resurrection will be an act of new creation. It will not be a simple return to the same sort of body as before; nor will it be a disembodied bliss. It will involve the gift of a new body with different properties.

9. This new identity is at present kept safe by God in heaven. At the moment of resurrection it will be brought from heaven to earth. Renewed bodies need a renewed earth. That is what the New Testament promises.

10. Early Christian belief splits the resurrection into two. For Paul, it takes place in two phases: first the Messiah; then his coming to all his people.

Key skills

Knowledge involves:

Selection of a range of (thorough) accurate and relevant information that is directly related to the specific demands of the question.

This means you choose the correct information relevant to the question set NOT the topic area. You will have to think and focus on selecting key information and NOT writing everything you know about the topic area.

Understanding involves:

Explanation that is extensive, demonstrating depth and/or breadth with excellent use of evidence and examples including (where appropriate) thorough and accurate supporting use of sacred texts, sources of wisdom and specialist language.

This means that you demonstrate that you understand something by being able to illustrate and expand your points through examples/supporting evidence in a personal way and NOT repeat chunks from a text book (known as rote learning).

Further application of skills:

Once you have made your choices and selected your information, compare them with another student. See if together you can decide on six and their correct order, this time, in sequence for answering a question.

Specification content

The historical reliability of the resurrection.

Issues for analysis and evaluation

The historical reliability of the resurrection

The historical reliability may be determined by one's acceptance or rejection of the alleged historical accounts of the resurrection in the Gospels. The relevant set text is John 20–21. How reliable is it?

The first thing to notice is that the events are described differently in Matthew, Mark and Luke. For example, in John's account, Mary Magdalene goes to the tomb alone; in the others, there are several other women. In John, no purpose for Mary's visit is given. In Matthew, the women go to 'look at' the tomb, while in Mark and Luke they bring spices to anoint Jesus' body. In John, Jesus appears to Mary Magdalene *after* she tells the disciples In Matthew; he appears to the women *before* they tell the disciples. In Mark, the women tell no one of what they had seen. John records resurrection appearance by Jesus in both Jerusalem and Galilee. In Matthew and Mark, the appearances are in Galilee, and Luke only records appearances in the vicinity of Jerusalem.

Some people might interpret these discrepancies as evidence of an unreliable testimony. The church, however, has always seen them as evidence of authenticity, representing various eyewitness traditions that are united on the main points.

Commentators have drawn attention to the highly structured nature of John's resurrection account. In chapter 20 we have a series of five episodes in which the risen Jesus overcomes the disciples' sorrow, fear and doubt to bring them to faith:

The five episodes form what is known as a chiasm. A chiasm is a style of writing that repeats similar ideas in reverse sequence (ABCBA). In the first and last, the risen Jesus does not appear, but people come to believe in the resurrection on the basis of evidence (the linen wrappings in verse 8, the testimony of others in verse 31). In the second and fourth episodes, Jesus appears to individuals (Mary and Thomas) who fail to recognise him. At the centre of the chiasm, he imparts the Holy Spirit to the disciples. Such a sophisticated literary device betrays more of a concern for theology than for historical objectivity.

John 21 raises further questions. For example, why are the disciples fishing in Galilee when they have been commissioned by Jesus and have received the Spirit?

Why do they still not recognise Jesus, having seen him twice in chapter 20? Why is the appearance described as the third, when there have already been three appearances in chapter 20? When the Gospel has come to a climax with Jesus' blessing on those who believe without having seen, what need is there for these further stories?

This has led some people to argue that John 21 is a later addition to the Gospel, probably written by John's disciples.

These questions may be answered as follows. John does not tell us why the disciples are back in Galilee, but other evangelists report that Jesus had told them to return there, where he would meet them. They may have gone fishing simply because they wanted to eat. The disciples' failure to recognise Jesus is consistent with the constant theme in John that there was something different about Jesus' resurrected body. John is counting Jesus' appearances to the disciples as a group, which excludes his appearance to Mary Magdalene. The aim of the stories is to allow Jesus to remind the disciples that they are entirely dependent upon him in the fulfilment of the commission that he has given them.

AO2 Activity *Possible lines of argument*

Listed below are some conclusions that could be drawn from the AO2 reasoning in the above text:

1. The Gospel accounts of the resurrection are totally unreliable.

2. The Gospel accounts of the resurrection are the work of the early church.

3. The Gospel accounts of the resurrection are reliable, eyewitness accounts.

Consider each of the conclusions drawn above and collect evidence and examples to support each argument from the AO1 and AO2 material studied in this section. Select one conclusion that you think is most convincing and explain why it is so. Now contrast this with the weakest conclusion in the list, justifying your argument with clear reasoning and evidence.

The nature of the resurrected body

Specification content
The nature of the resurrected body.

His followers obviously recognise who the resurrected Jesus is. Yet, the nature of his resurrected body, as described in the Gospels, obviously differs so much from that of his earthly body that they sometimes have difficulty in identifying him. He seems to be able to appear and vanish at will and to pass through locked doors, and yet he is no ghostly apparition because the disciples can see and touch his wounds; he takes food and cooks breakfast.

Paul, in 1 Corinthians 15, discusses the question with what kind of body the dead are raised. His teaching may appear confused. He gives no indication of how or when this change will be brought about. He writes of a 'spiritual body', which is a contradiction in terms and suggests a spiritual rather than a physical resurrection. This is not what the early Christians believed.

However, Paul is clear that there will be a bodily resurrection. The resurrected body will be imperishable, glorious, strong. It will be 'spiritual' (*pneumatikos*), in the sense that it will not be subject to death. It will be different from the earthly body, which is perishable, dishonourable, weak and subject to death. We cannot predict exactly what the resurrected body will be like any more than we can predict what will grow from some unfamiliar seed. There will, however, be continuity as well as change. The old body will not be totally abandoned, nor will it be totally kept. In this Paul echoes the New Testament accounts of the risen Jesus, whose body seems to have undergone a significant change.

The nature of the resurrected body has been long debated in the Christian church. Irenaeus, for instance, re-iterates Paul's view when he writes 'Against Heresies' and states that 'although dispersed throughout the whole world' the church has 'received from the apostles and from their disciples the faith in ... the raising up again of all flesh of all humanity.' Indeed, the Roman Catholic stance, stated in the *Catechism of the Catholic Church* is that 'We believe in the true resurrection of this flesh that we now possess'. In general, most Christian beliefs would agree that the nature of the resurrected body is difficult to explain but that it is somehow the same earthly body that is 'glorified' or given a newly defined spiritual status. In this sense, the church appears to replicate the vague depiction (nature of the resurrected body) of an accepted certainty (that the body will be resurrected) that can be found in the Bible itself.

It could be argued that the resurrected is the same earthly body but in a rejuvenated form. For example, people often speak of being in their 'prime' at one point during life and then later, getting older the body becomes weak. But this does not mean it is a different body and no one would suggest that it is essentially different. Therefore, the same physical body 'glorified' could mean something like this, that is, the same body but in its greatest possible form?

In conclusion, it may be unsatisfactory, but maybe one possible position to take is to accept that the 'mystery' of the resurrection extends beyond the act itself to that of questions pertaining to the nature of the resurrected body?

AO2 Activity *Possible lines of argument*

Listed below are some conclusions that could be drawn from the AO2 reasoning in the above text:

1. The resurrection body is no different from the earthly body.

2. The resurrection body is a 'spiritual body'.

3. The resurrection body is a transformed body.

Consider each of the conclusions drawn above and collect evidence and examples to support each argument from the AO1 and AO2 material studied in this section. Select one conclusion that you think is most convincing and explain why it is so. Now contrast this with the weakest conclusion in the list, justifying your argument with clear reasoning and evidence.

Key skills

Analysis involves identifying issues raised by the materials in the AO1, together with those identified in the AO2 section, and presents sustained and clear views, either of scholars or from a personal perspective ready for evaluation.

This means that it picks out key things to debate and the lines of argument presented by others or a personal point of view.

Evaluation involves considering the various implications of the issues raised based upon the evidence gleaned from analysis and provides an extensive detailed argument with a clear conclusion.

This means that the answer weighs up the various and different lines of argument analysed through individual commentary and response and arrives at a conclusion through a clear process of reasoning.

AO2 Developing skills

It is now time to reflect upon the information that has been covered so far. It is also important to consider how what you have learned can be focused and used for examination-style answers by practising the skills associated with AO2.

Assessment objective 2 (AO2) involves 'analysis' and 'evaluation'. The terms may be obvious but it is crucial to be familiar with how certain skills demonstrate these terms, and also, how the performance of these skills is measured (see generic band descriptors Band 5 for AS AO2).

Obviously, an answer is placed within an appropriate band descriptor depending upon how well the answer performs, ranging from excellent, good, satisfactory, basic/limited to very limited.

▶ **Your task is this:** from the list of the ten key points below, select six that are relevant to the evaluation task below. Put your selection into an order that you would use to address the task set. In explaining why you have chosen these six to answer the task, you will find that you are developing a process of reasoning. This will help you to develop an argument to decide whether or not the Gospel accounts of the resurrection of Jesus are historically true.

'The Gospel accounts of the resurrection of Jesus are historically true.' Assess/evaluate this view.

1. The early Christians believed that Jesus was the Messiah.

2. They believed this despite the fact that he had not achieved what the Messiah was supposed to achieve.

3. They believed it because they believed that Jesus had risen from the dead.

4. Other Jewish leaders had promised that they would be resurrected, but nobody believed that they had been, for the obvious reason that they had not.

5. The Gospel accounts of the resurrection are not simply a way of talking about him 'going to Heaven when he died'. It was forty days after the resurrection that he was exalted to heaven.

6. The risen Jesus invites the disciples to touch him to make sure he is a real human being. At the same time, he appears and disappears, sometimes through locked doors. The evangelists are telling, with bewilderment, stories about how Jesus' body was now different.

7. However, some people would say that Jesus somehow survived the crucifixion.

8. Others might argue that the tomb was empty, but there had been no resurrection.

9. Again, others might think that the disciples simply had visions of Jesus.

10. If so, would the disciples have spent the rest of their lives preaching what they knew to be a lie?

C: The Bible as a source of wisdom and authority in daily life

Make sure you have read and understood the set texts:
Ecclesiastes 12:13–14; Luke 6:36–37; Psalm 119:9–16;
Psalm 119:105–112; Genesis 1:26–28; Ecclesiastes 9:5–9;
Psalm 46:1–3; Matthew 6:25.

What is the Christian Bible?

The English word 'bible' comes from the Greek words *tà biblía:* 'the books'. The Christian Bible is a collection of sacred books bound together in two volumes known as the Old Testament and the New Testament.

The Old Testament was written originally in Hebrew. It is the sacred scripture of the Jewish religion as well as being sacred to Christians. Protestant Bibles have 39 Old Testament books, the same as in the Hebrew Bible. Catholic and Orthodox Bibles have 46, because they include other books, known collectively as the Apocrypha, which Protestants consider to be **deuterocanonical**.

The Old Testament was written and edited by many authors over a period of many centuries. It tells the story of God's engagement with the people of Israel from the earliest times until their return to Jerusalem from exile in Babylon in 538 BCE. It is worth remembering that it was the Bible used by Jesus.

Key quote

The New Testament lies hidden in the Old, and the Old Testament is unveiled in the New. (St Augustine)

The New Testament was written originally in Greek. It has 27 books, each one focusing on Jesus. There are:

- Four Gospels (Matthew, Mark, Luke and John), which tell the story of Jesus' life and ministry.
- The Book of *Acts*, which records the founding of the early church.
- A collection of 21 *Epistles* (letters) to various churches, 14 of them written by Paul (although there is a strong doubt amongst scholars that Paul actually wrote all 14).
- A book of visions, known as the Book of *Revelations*, by an early church leader.

The Bible can be read in many ways: as great poetry, as a law book or a history book, or as a basis for theological reflection. For Christians, however, its main aim is practical. You will recall that the Gospel of John (20:31) identified that aim as follows:

'these [things] are written so that you may come to believe that Jesus is the Messiah, the Son of God, and that through believing you may have life in his name.'

Christians believe that the Bible gives instruction on the meaning and purpose of life, and that it is both a guide to everyday living and a source of comfort and encouragement.

This section covers AO1 content and skills

Specification content

The ways in which the Bible is considered authoritative: as a source of moral advice

(Ecclesiastes 12:13–14; Luke 6:36–37); as a guide to living (Psalm 119:9–16; Psalm 119:105–112); as teaching on the meaning and purpose of life (Genesis 1:26–28; Ecclesiastes 9:5–9); and as a source of comfort and encouragement (Psalm 46:1–3; Matthew 6:25).

quickfire

1.13 What is the origin of the English word *'bible'*?

Key term

Deuterocanonical: a second list of sacred books considered to be genuine

The Old Testament was originally written in Hebrew

The Bible's teaching on the meaning and purpose of life

The Bible is not a systematic essay on the meaning and purpose and life. It is rather an account of how God dealt with a variety of different people over a period of centuries. It tells the story of God's plan to save human beings from sin. This story is known as 'salvation history', and may be summarised as follows:

- The Bible begins with an account of how God created the universe. In creating human beings, Genesis states that God says: 'Let us make mankind in our image, in our likeness, so that they may rule over the fish in the sea and the birds in the sky, over the livestock and all the wild animals, and over all the creatures that move along the ground.' The purpose of human beings, first and foremost, was to be the pinnacle of God's creation and, for many Christians, rulers and maintainers of the created order.

- Everything was good, until Adam and Eve, the first man and woman, disobeyed God and brought sin and death to the world. Their disobedience is known as the Fall. Their sin, known as original sin, is passed on to all generations. God, however, had always had a plan to save his people.

- God makes a covenant with a man named Abraham that he will have countless descendants who will inherit a Promised Land. Abraham's twelve great-grandsons become the founding fathers (known as 'the patriarchs') of the Twelve Tribes of Israel and the ancestors of the Jewish faith.

- The Israelites become slaves in Egypt, but God calls Moses to liberate them. Their escape and the subsequent forty years they spend in the wilderness is known as 'the Exodus'. During this time, a key event occurs when God makes a covenant with Moses and gives him the Law, summarised in the Ten Commandments, which the Israelites must obey.

- Moses dies, and the Israelite conquest of the Promised Land is led by Joshua, who divides the land between the Twelve Tribes. A pattern develops: the people are unfaithful to God; they are conquered by their enemies; they cry to God for help; God chooses men and women called 'judges' to lead them to victory; everything is fine until the cycle begins again.

- Saul is anointed first King of Israel, but is beset by personal difficulties and is eventually succeeded by his son-in-law, David. Under David and his son, Solomon, Israel becomes a mighty empire with Jerusalem as its capital city, but both David and Solomon succumb to many temptations, and after Solomon's death, the kingdom splits into two – Israel in the north and Judah in the south. In both kingdoms, most of the kings are unfaithful to God, but God calls prophets, such as Amos, Hosea and Isaiah, to summon the people to faithfulness.

- As the people are still disobedient, God lets the Assyrians conquer Israel in 721 BCE, and the Babylonians conquer Judah in 587 BCE. The people of Judah, now known as 'Judeans' or 'Jews', spend fifty years in captivity in Babylon, a period known as 'the Exile'. They return to Judah, to rebuild Jerusalem and the Temple. The Old Testament story ends here.

- The story continues in the Apocrypha. Judah is conquered by the Greeks. Around 150 BCE, the Maccabees lead a successful revolt to restore Jewish independence. New Jewish religious groups, such as the Essenes, the Pharisees and the Sadducees, arise during this time.

Key terms

Covenant: an agreement between God and his people

Original sin: the sin of Adam and Eve, which all human beings inherit

---

quickfire

1.14 What is *original sin*?

Key quote

How can a young person stay on the path of purity? By living according to your word. (Psalm 119:9)

Key quote

Your word is a lamp for my feet, a light on my path. (Psalm 119:105)

Key quote

Now all has been heard;
here is the conclusion of the matter:
Fear God and keep his commandments,
for this is the duty of all mankind.
For God will bring every deed into judgment,
including every hidden thing,
whether it is good or evil.
(Ecclesiastes 12:13–14)

- In addition to the history of the Israelite people, the Old Testament contains examples of their laws, their poetry and their wisdom. The Book of Psalms is a collection of poems, many of them (e.g. Psalm 46:1–3) expressing faith in God, others offering a guide to living (Psalm 119:9–16; Psalm 119:105–112). The author of the Book of Ecclesiastes meditates on the best way to live (9:5–9) in the face of an impending and unavoidable death and offers moral advice (12:13–14).

- Ecclesiastes 9: 7–9 brings with it a positive message for all to enjoy life: 'Go, eat your food with gladness, and drink your wine with a joyful heart, for God has already approved what you do … Enjoy life with your wife, whom you love, all the days of this meaningless life that God has given you under the sun – all your meaningless days. For this is your lot in life and in your toilsome labour under the sun.'

- The New Testament takes up the story. Judah has by now been conquered again, this time by the Romans. But God does not abandon his people. He sends his only Son, Jesus Christ, into the world. During his public ministry Jesus preaches love and forgiveness (e.g. Luke 6:36–37) and that salvation comes through faith, not through political power. His disciples realise that he is the Messiah, the Saviour for whom the Jews had long been waiting, but when Jesus is crucified by his enemies, they think that all is lost. After three days, however, God raises Jesus from the dead, thus affirming that he is the Son of God. New Testament writers realise that sin and death are now conquered forever because those who believe in Jesus will share his resurrection. God's original plan for his creation is thus brought full circle.

- The final part of the New Testament tells what happened after the Holy Spirit descended on the disciples to give them the courage to preach about Jesus, first to the Jews and then, led by Paul, to the Gentiles as well. Many Christian communities were set up. In a short space of time Christianity spread throughout the Roman Empire.

For Christians, the Bible story teaches men and women that there is more to life than food and clothing (Matthew 6:25). They can find no meaning in life apart from God, because God is life. Every single person has been created in the image of God, and created for eternity.

Above all, the meaning of life is to be found in Jesus, the Son of God, who said of himself, 'I am the way, and the truth and the life' (John 14:6). According to John (17:3), Jesus also said 'And this is eternal life, that they may know you, the only true God, and Jesus Christ whom you have sent'.

Therefore, the purpose of human life is to find God, to know him, to do his will, to serve him, to obey him and to show him to the world. It is to worship God and to give him the glory that is due to him. Christians believe that those who believe in Jesus will share his resurrection and eventually receive the ultimate reward of eternal life.

AO1 Activity

Research further, what we know about the formation and compilation of the Bible.

Specific knowledge and details gleaned from this will serve to fuel evidence and examples for both a demonstration of knowledge and understanding (AO1) but also to help sustain an argument (AO2).

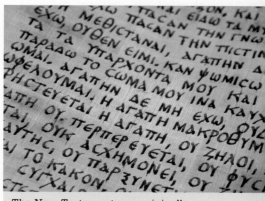

The New Testament was originally written in Greek

Key quote

Then God said,

'Let us make humankind in our image, according to our likeness; and let them have dominion over the fish of the sea, and over the birds of the air, and over the cattle, and over all the wild animals of the earth, and over every creeping thing that creeps upon the earth.' So God created humankind in his image, in the image of God he created them; male and female he created them. God blessed them, and God said to them, 'Be fruitful and multiply, and fill the earth and subdue it; and have dominion over the fish of the sea and over the birds of the air and over every living thing that moves upon the earth.'
(Genesis 1:26–28)

Key quote

If Christ has not been raised, your faith is futile.
(I Corinthians 15:17)

The Bible as a guide to everyday living

The Bible's primary purpose is practical and dynamic. It aims to guide readers in their daily living. The Old Testament is full of religious laws but it also has more general 'guides' as to how to behave. For example, read Psalm 119:9–16 and Psalm 119:105–112, as an example for Christians of a guide to living.

Christians believe that it does this by pointing people to Jesus. 'You search the scriptures,' Jesus told the Jews, 'because you think that in them you have eternal life; and it is they that testify on my behalf' (John 5:39). The true guide to Christian living is therefore not the Bible but Jesus himself.

Christians are saved not through their behaviour but through faith in Jesus. True faith, however, will result in a special kind of behaviour inspired not by the fear of punishment but by love for God. If human beings love God, Jesus will live in them and lead them through the Holy Spirit to obedience. And when they fail, they can repent and ask for forgiveness, which they know will be given to them.

Jesus did not issue his followers a set of detailed regulations for daily living, but he set an example. The Christian life is therefore to show loyalty to Jesus by rejecting selfish desire and following him in his obedience to God, his prayerful humility, his kindness to the poor and disadvantaged and marginalised, his service to others. The Christian does as Jesus did.

What then about Old Testament Law? Are Christians bound by the Law of Moses? Once again, the key is to follow Jesus.

In the Sermon on the Mount (Matthew 5:17–18) Jesus says that he has come not to abolish the Law of Moses but to fulfil it. This seems to suggest that the Law of Moses is meant to last for ever. He then goes on to tell his followers that unless their righteousness exceeds that of the scribes and Pharisees, precisely those members of Jewish society who adhered most strictly to the Law, they will not enter the kingdom of heaven. He quotes six of God's commandments (on murder, adultery, divorce, swearing oaths, retaliation, loving a neighbour) showing how the scribes and Pharisees interpreted each one, and then revealing God's true intent in each case.

> ## Study tip
>
> Read how and why Jesus broke the Pharasaic Law in Matthew 12:10; 15:1–3; Luke 6:1–4.

Jesus objected not to the Law itself, but to mistaken interpretations of the Law by the Pharisees and others. He tells his listeners that they are to be perfect, 'as your heavenly Father is perfect'. He demands from his followers a higher degree of holiness. They must obey not the letter but the spirit of the Law. It is not only their actions that need to be right, but their motives as well.

Christians who follow Jesus are not required to follow the Jewish Law on minor issues such as ritual or dietary regulations. This was made clear at the Council of Jerusalem (Acts 15), when it was decided that Gentile Christians did not have to succumb to all the rigours of the Law of Moses. Christians are called to be free. Perfect freedom, however, comes only through obedience to God's will.

> ## AO1 Activity
>
> Read Psalm 119:9–16 and Psalm 119:105–112. State three ways from each passage that would guide and instruct Christians in how to live.

The Bible as a source of comfort and encouragement

St Paul in his Epistle to the Romans 15:4 writes that the Holy Scriptures have been written 'for our instruction, so that by steadfastness and by the encouragement of the scriptures we might have hope'.

The Bible is a source of comfort and encouragement. Because it deals with the timeless elements of human nature, it portrays men and women with whose hopes and failures Christians in all ages can identify. It also portrays a God whose love for human beings does not change from age to age.

The human condition is fundamentally the same today as it was in biblical times. People still struggle with the same difficulties as their forebears – temptation, sin, bereavement, poverty, conflict, the fear of death. The Bible has something to say on all these things:

- On temptation and sin, it teaches that even the most devout people, e.g. King David, may fail from time to time, but if there is repentance, God will readily forgive.

- On bereavement, it teaches that death is not the end. In John 11:11 Jesus tells the disciples that his departed friend, Lazarus, 'has fallen asleep, but I am going … to awaken him'. Jesus then raised Lazarus to life. Christians believe that death is only temporary and that everyone who dies will be 'awakened' in God's good time.

- On poverty, it teaches that the poor are to be treated equitably. Jesus understood the reality of poverty and stressed the need to give to the poor and to provide for them. He identified with poor people and, like many of them, did not have a home. He taught how difficult it was for a rich person to inherit the kingdom of heaven.

- On suffering, it teaches that suffering, when handled joyfully, can be a testimony to the character of Jesus. Suffering can help people to maintain a spirit of humility, to learn to sympathise with others and to rely on God's promises. It is a test of their loyalty.

- On the fear of death, it teaches that Jesus has conquered death so that human beings who believe in him may share in his resurrection.

The Bible therefore offers comfort to believers on grief arising from temptation and sin, bereavement, poverty, suffering and death.

AO1 Activity

Read Psalm 46:1–3 and Matthew 6:25. Explain how you think these verses may help Christians in living their lives when times are difficult.

Key quotes

Therefore I tell you, do not worry about your life, what you will eat or drink; or about your body, what you will wear. Is not life more than food, and the body more than clothes? (Matthew 6:25)

God is our refuge and strength, an ever-present help in trouble. Therefore we will not fear, though the earth give way and the mountains fall into the heart of the sea, though its waters roar and foam and the mountains quake with their surging. (Psalm 46:1–3)

quickfire

1.15 Why, according to St Paul, have the Holy Scriptures been written?

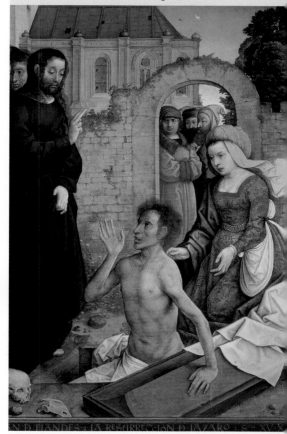

Juan de Flandes: The Raising of Lazarus

Key skills

Knowledge involves:

Selection of a range of (thorough) accurate and relevant information that is directly related to the specific demands of the question.

This means you choose the correct information relevant to the question set NOT the topic area. You will have to think and focus on selecting key information and NOT writing everything you know about the topic area.

Understanding involves:

Explanation that is extensive, demonstrating depth and/or breadth with excellent use of evidence and examples including (where appropriate) thorough and accurate supporting use of sacred texts, sources of wisdom and specialist language.

This means that you demonstrate that you understand something by being able to illustrate and expand your points through examples/supporting evidence in a personal way and NOT repeat chunks from a text book (known as rote learning).

Further application of skills:

Why not explore some further selections from the Bible that can be used as examples for authority and wisdom. The Book of Proverbs and the Book of Ecclesiastes in the Old Testament are good examples.

AO1 Developing skills

It is now time to reflect upon the information that has been covered so far. It is also important to consider how what you have learned can be focused and used for examination-style answers by practising the skills associated with AO1.

Assessment objective 1 (AO1) involves demonstrating knowledge and understanding. The terms 'knowledge' and 'understanding' are obvious but it is crucial to be familiar with how certain skills demonstrate these terms, and also, how the performance of these skills is measured (see generic band descriptors Band 5 for AS AO1).

▶ **Your new task is this:** you need to develop each of the key points below by adding evidence and examples to fully explain each point. The first one is done for you. This will help you in answering examination questions for AO1 by being able to 'demonstrate extensive depth and/or breadth' with 'excellent use of evidence and examples' (Level 5 AO1 band descriptor).

1. The Bible can be read in many ways.

DEVELOPMENT: *For example, the Bible is a source of comfort and encouragement because it portrays men and women with whose hopes and failures Christians in all ages can identify.*

2. The Bible is not a systematic essay on the meaning and purpose and life. It is rather an account of ...

3. The Old Testament tells the story of ...

4. The New Testament tells the story of ...

5. According to the Bible, the purpose of life is ...

6. Paul, in his Letter to the Romans, wrote that the Holy Scripture 'is written for ...'

Issues for analysis and evaluation

The relative value of the Bible as teaching on the meaning and purpose of life

Specification content

The relative value of the bible as teaching on the meaning and purpose of life.

One could argue that the Bible contains several different messages about the meaning of life: for instance, it gives meaning to the origins of life by way of a creation narrative; it also provides meaning through a historical and theological overview of life so far; this then culminates in a specific story of salvation, through Jesus, for human beings; finally, it has hope for a future existence through resurrection of the dead. However, many Christians have argued that these different aspects all contribute to making sense of the greater picture of the meaning of life as a whole. Some Christians would say that this all works together as a grand narrative in explaining the meaning of life.

This explanation certainly gives answers for both individual Christians and the Christian community as a whole, which is arguably of great value for a religious believer in that it satisfies curiosity about ultimate questions and provides a sense of direction and security in life. This inevitably then leads to questions about their purpose in life. Indeed, the purpose of life is seen by most Christians as summarised by Jesus' Greatest Commandment to 'love God' and demonstrate 'love for neighbour' in Luke chapter 10 which, in practice, has many implications. To worship God and follow God's guidance is one aspect of this, as the Psalm 119 says, 'Your word is a lamp for my feet, a light on my path.' In this sense Christians believe that they are reflecting the 'image' and 'likeness' of their creator. Christians are encouraged to 'Fear God and keep his commandments' (Ecclesiastes 12). Therefore, at the same time, in conjunction with an awareness of others through a moral life Christians have, arguably, the complete picture for the meaning and purpose in life. This understanding then supports the view that the Bible is indeed of great value for Christians.

It could even be argued that the 'love for neighbour' extends beyond Christianity in that there is often parity between secular ideas of enjoyment of life, awareness of others through society and an equal passion to work towards challenging social injustices. In addition, there is also the consideration that the Bible maintains some authority with regard to meaning and purpose in society today as reflected in the underpinning principles behind the justice system and, for example, Sunday trading laws. It could be argued, then, that the Bible has great relevance for the purposes of life today even beyond the Christian community.

Nonetheless, despite this, the relative value of the Bible in providing answers to the meaning of life could be challenged; for example, the existence of a creator God is often questioned and the theory of evolution through survival of the fittest challenges the effectiveness of the greater picture. Indeed, the theological story underpinning the Bible can be seen as inconsistent, puzzling and also raises crucial questions about the nature of God in light of such realities as suffering.

In conclusion, the Bible appears to have great value for Christians in terms of the meaning and purpose of life, although this is relative to whether or not a believer is affected by the challenges brought about by questions as to the credibility of an explanation of a creator God. In terms of a more secular understanding of the meaning of life, it appears that the Bible has less value today. Despite this, the Bible is still seen as the best-selling book in the world and yet, arguably, also the least read best-selling book in the world!

AO2 Activity *Possible lines of argument*

Listed below are some conclusions that could be drawn from the AO2 reasoning in the accompanying text:

1. The Bible has little value as a guide to the meaning and purpose of life today as the idea of a creator God is questioned by many.

2. The Bible only has value for Christians in terms of the meaning and purpose of life.

3. The Bible still is of great value today in relation to the meaning and purpose of life despite challenges made against the idea of a creator God.

Consider each of the conclusions drawn above and collect evidence and examples to support each argument from the AO1 and AO2 material studied in this section. Select one conclusion that you think is most convincing and explain why it is so. Now contrast this with the weakest conclusion in the list, justifying your argument with clear reasoning and evidence.

Specification content

The extent to which the Psalms studied offer a guide to living for Christians.

The extent to which the Psalms studied offer a guide to living for Christians

Some may argue that the world of the Psalms is very far removed from the reality of 21st-century life. It is difficult to relate to many of the strange rites and customs that they reflect (temple worship and sacrifice, for example). Today, we live in a scientific age when people are more educated, liberated and enlightened than those for whom the Psalms were originally written. For example, the scientific theory of evolution has disproved the biblical version of creation, which the Psalms take for granted.

Indeed, one has to consider their purpose and the original historical context of the Psalms, which were designed for use in the Temple cult in Jerusalem during the Hebrew monarchy, and were then reinterpreted to suit the needs of Judaism. Some would suggest that this demonstrates that they have nothing to offer as a guide to living for Christians.

However, an alternative perspective and argument could be that although their scientific ideas may be out of date, the Psalms were not written as a textbook of science or history but to present fundamental truths about God in order to bring about a change in the reader's life. They offer comfort to those who are worried about sin, suffering and death. Some of them even foreshadow the key belief in the resurrection, which gives Christian believers a meaning, and purpose in life.

In support of this argument, the Psalms address timeless questions that have not changed much over the centuries, e.g. why am I here? What is God like? Why does evil prosper while the good suffer? Is there any hope for human beings? In that sense, they speak to every faith and to every age. They often contain sublime poetry that stirs our emotions. They discuss deep, philosophical questions about life, death and eternity.

More pertinent to the issue is that they instruct the believer to follow God's 'word': 'How can a young person stay on the path of purity? By living according to your word.' (Psalm 119:9). God's word is, according to Psalm 119:105, 'a lamp for my feet, a light on my path'.

Such advice is clear, although some may say it is not precise enough as a guide to life and would criticise the vagueness of the directions contained in the Psalms in terms of specific moral and social duties. However, since they were not meant to be a social or moral textbook, some would see this as an unfair criticism.

In conclusion, it could be argued that the Psalms provide clear and direct instruction to follow God's word and inspirational verses to encourage this, for example, Psalm 119:109–112 which reads:

'Though I constantly take my life in my hands, I will not forget your law.
The wicked have set a snare for me, but I have not strayed from your precepts.
Your statutes are my heritage forever; they are the joy of my heart.
My heart is set on keeping your decrees to the very end.'

However, it may have to be accepted that they are to be seen in partnership with other biblical texts, if the specific nature of that instruction is to be understood fully, and offer a guide for living for a Christian in practical terms.

AO2 Activity *Possible lines of argument*

Listed below are some conclusions that could be drawn from the AO2 reasoning in the accompanying text:

1. The Psalms are worthless as a guide to living for Christians.

2. The Psalms have some value as a guide to living for Christians.

3. The Psalms offer a comprehensive guide to living for Christians.

Consider each of the conclusions drawn above and collect evidence and examples to support each argument from the AO1 and AO2 material studied in this section. Select one conclusion that you think is most convincing and explain why it is so. Now contrast this with the weakest conclusion in the list, justifying your argument with clear reasoning and evidence.

AO2 Developing skills

It is now time to reflect upon the information that has been covered so far. It is also important to consider how what you have learned can be focused and used for examination-style answers by practising the skills associated with AO2.

Assessment objective 2 (AO2) involves 'analysis' and 'evaluation'. The terms may be obvious but it is crucial to be familiar with how certain skills demonstrate these terms, and also, how the performance of these skills is measured (see generic band descriptors Band 5 for AS AO2).

Obviously an answer is placed within an appropriate band descriptor depending upon how well the answer performs, ranging from excellent, good, satisfactory, basic/limited to very limited.

▶ **Your next task is this:** develop each of the key points below by adding evidence and examples to fully evaluate the argument presented in the evaluation statement. The first one is done for you. This will help you in answering examination questions for AO2 by being able to ensure that 'sustained and clear views are given, supported by extensive, detailed reasoning and/or evidence' (Level 5 AO2 band descriptor).

An evaluation statement that deals with the Bible as the word of God and providing complete guidance for Christians.

1. Some argue that the Bible is the inspired word of God.

DEVELOPMENT: *The Bible's 66 books, written by many different authors over many centuries, have a common theme – the redemption of God's people. It claims itself that it is the word of God for 'teaching, rebuking, correcting and training in righteousness' (2 Timothy 3:16). Like God himself, it is inerrant and authoritative. Its message is eternal for all peoples of all times.*

2. Christian theology teaches that Jesus, not the Bible, is the word of God.

3. The Bible does not deal with modern issues directly. Therefore, it is not complete in detail even if it is complete in guidance.

4. The Bible is interpreted differently by different scholars. Therefore, it cannot give complete guidance.

5. The Bible deals with religion and morality and is therefore a complete guide for life today.

6. The historical context of the Bible limits its relevance today because society today is very different from that of Old and New Testament times.

Key skills

Analysis involves identifying issues raised by the materials in the AO1, together with those identified in the AO2 section, and presents sustained and clear views, either of scholars or from a personal perspective ready for evaluation.

This means that it picks out key things to debate and the lines of argument presented by others or a personal point of view.

Evaluation involves considering the various implications of the issues raised based upon the evidence gleaned from analysis and provides an extensive detailed argument with a clear conclusion.

This means that the answer weighs up the various and different lines of argument analysed through individual commentary and response and arrives at a conclusion through a clear process of reasoning.

T2 Religious concepts

Specification content

Is God male? The issue of male language about God; the pastoral benefits and challenges of the model of Father; Sallie McFague and God as mother.

A: The Nature of God

Is God male?

The original languages of the Bible (Hebrew and Greek) consistently speak of God as 'Father'. They also refer to God by the masculine personal pronoun 'he'. Jesus, the Son of God, is a male, and the Holy Spirit of God is traditionally spoken of as a 'he'.

God is likened to a human father. He provides for his children, disciplines them and loves them. This does not, however, mean that he is a male, any more than referring to 'Mother Earth' means that the earth is a female. God exists in a form that defies male and female categories.

Jesus is spoken of as the 'Son of God' and the 'Son of Man'. During his life on earth, he was clearly a man. However, Christians believe that before he ever became incarnate he was 'with God and was God' (John 1:1), and therefore was neither male nor female.

The Bible consistently refers to the Holy Spirit in masculine terms, as a person with insight, knowledge and a will, who can be lied to, grieved and insulted. This does not mean that the Holy Spirit is a male, however. As the name implies, he is a spirit.

God as Father

In the New Testament, God's fatherhood conveys two distinct ideas:

1. God as Creator of the world (John 1:3 implies Jesus was creator as well).
2. The relationship between God and Jesus. Jesus called God 'Father' and taught his disciples to do the same. The term conveys an approachable and personal deity.

The title 'Father', therefore, suggests two different characteristics of God: his lordship over creation and his loving kindness.

There are also several passages in the Bible that portray God in female terms. In Isaiah 66:13, for example, God is described as a comforting mother. In Matthew 23:37 (Luke 13:34), Jesus uses a motherly illustration of himself, and in Luke 15:8–10, he compares God to a woman searching for a lost coin.

However, the Bible is absolutely clear that God is neither male nor female. Jesus himself said: 'God is spirit' (John 4:24). He can identify with the needs of all people, male and female, because he created them in his own image: 'male and female he created them' (Genesis 1:27). As Paul wrote in his Epistle to the Galatians (3:28): 'there is no longer male and female, for all of you are one in Christ Jesus'.

Study tip

Find some more female images of God in the Bible and be ready to use them as evidence and examples in an answer.

Although the Bible is clear that God values both men and women equally, some theologians have expressed concern about its consistent use of male language about God.

Key quote

As a father has compassion for his children, so the Lord has compassion for those who fear him. (Psalm 103:13–14)

quickfire

2.1 What two characteristics of God does the title 'Father' convey?

Key quote

O Jerusalem, Jerusalem! … How often have I desired to gather your children together as a hen gathers her brood under her wings, and you were not willing! (Matthew 23:34)

Study tip

Note that the correct term for one who studies theology is **theologian** (not 'theologist').

Sallie McFague: God as Mother

Sallie McFague is an American theologian who writes from an ecofeminist perspective.

In her *Metaphorical Theology: Models of God in Religious Language* (1982) she maintains that all language about God is metaphorical. Names and titles ('father', 'king', etc.) are simply ways in which we think about God. They say very little about God's true nature.

The metaphors used often turn into idols: we end up worshipping the metaphor instead of God. However, all metaphors miss the mark and many metaphors become outdated with time.

McFague wants to provide new metaphors for understanding God in ways that are meaningful today.

By using the metaphor of God as Mother, she is not saying that God is a Mother (or even female) but that the image of 'mother' highlights certain characteristics of God (such as love for the world).

McFague develops a metaphor of the world as God's body.

She goes on to develop three metaphors for God's relationship with the world. The metaphors correspond to three Christian doctrines, three ethical elements and three types of love:

1. *Mother*: corresponding to the traditional title, 'Father'; the doctrine of creation; the ethical element of justice; and *agape* love (selfless love), the type of love God has for the world.

2. *Lover*: corresponding to the traditional title 'Son'; the doctrine of salvation; the ethical element of healing; and *eros* (desire), the way in which God's love works in the world.

3. *Friend*: corresponding to the traditional title 'Spirit'; the doctrine of eschatology; the ethical element of companionship; and *philia* (companionship), the way in which humans should interact in the world.

According to McFague, masculine language conveying God's unilateral, sovereign rule has led to the abuse of the natural world and the domination of women by men. If God is called 'Mother', it follows that the world is no longer ruled over by God, but is part of God's body or womb. So to harm nature is to harm God. This belief is known as panentheism.

McFague argues that maternal images of God 'giving birth, nursing, comforting, and caring' highlight humanity's complete reliance on God.

It is important, however, that God should be imagined in female, not feminine terms, because 'the first refers to gender while the second refers to qualities conventionally associated with women. ... Thus, the feminine side of God is taken to comprise the tender, nurturing, passive, healing aspects of divine activity, whereas those activities in which God creates, redeems, establishes peace, administers justice, and so on, are called masculine'.

Key terms

Ecofeminist: someone who is interested in both the environment and women's rights

Metaphor: something that represents or is a symbol for something else

Panentheism: the belief that the universe is the visible part of God

Key person

Sallie McFague (born 1933): an American theologian who sees the earth as 'God's body'.

Sallie McFague

She also warns against sentimentalising maternal imagery. We cannot suppose that mothers are 'naturally' loving, comforting or self-sacrificing. These qualities are in fact social constructions: society wants women to think that they are biologically programmed to be these things. Rather, the metaphor of God as mother focuses 'on the most basic things that females (as mothers) do: ... give birth, feed and protect the young, want the young to flourish'.

While some theologians have welcomed McFague's concept of God as mother, others have rejected it as unbiblical. Jesus asserted that God was 'Father'. If he was wrong on this fundamental point, how can we trust him on anything? Moreover, in specific relation to Jesus, the terms 'father' and 'mother' are not interchangeable terms, because clearly Jesus' mother was Mary.

> ### AO1 Activity
>
> Someone asks you what Sallie McFague has to say about God as Mother. Write down what your answer would be in 200 words. If you are doing this a group, read out your answers. Take three examples and try to make one final version by extracting what is the best material from each one.

Can God suffer?

The traditional Christian view

Traditional Christian theology has always proclaimed the impassibility of God.

'Impassibility' (from Latin *in* = not + *passibilis* = able to suffer or experience emotion) is the English word used to translate the Greek *apatheia* (from *a* = without + *pathos* = suffering). Its first meaning is 'unable to suffer'. An extended meaning is 'incapable of emotion of any kind'. It asserts that God is unable to experience emotion or suffering or pain, and therefore has no feelings that are analogous to human feelings. This attribute is closely related to God's immutability (his unchanging nature).

The Old Testament reveals a God who is omniscient, omnipotent and omnibenevolent, and transcends all that exists, the 'Wholly Other'. Nothing can cause a change in his inner emotional state. While he displays a range of emotions – love, grief, compassion, anger, etc. – which often cause him to 'repent' or 'change his mind', he consistently acts with compassion and mercy.

The New Testament reveals a God who has become incarnate in Jesus. Jesus, in his human nature, is passible: he is able to feel emotion and pain, particularly in his passion and cross. This does not, however, affect the impassibility of his divine nature: it has always been God's plan to overcome the suffering with resurrection.

Over the last century or so, several prominent theologians have challenged this traditional view of God. In response to a conviction that after two world wars, the Jewish holocaust, and continuing conflicts and genocides, Christians cannot have faith in a God who is immune to suffering, they argue that God is passible, that he does undergo emotional change and that he can suffer.

> ### Study tip
>
> Candidates are often good at remembering key points but sometimes they do not explain them fully. For development of a point, bring in a variety of ways in which the application of this point is demonstrated and introduce some contrasting scholarly views if possible to help support your answer. This shows that the answer 'demonstrates extensive depth and/or breadth. Excellent use of evidence and examples' (L5 band descriptor AO1), as opposed to the information being simply 'limited in depth and/or breadth, including limited use of evidence and examples' (L2 band descriptor AO1).

quickfire

2.2 What are the female (as opposed to the feminine) characteristics of God?

Specification content

Can God suffer? The impassibility of God; the modern view of a suffering God illustrated by Jürgen Moltmann (*The Crucified Christ*).

quickfire

2.3 What is meant by God's:
 a. impassibility?
 b. immutability?

Key terms

Immutability: unchangeable

Impassibility: having no human feelings

Omnibenevolent: all good

Omnipotent: all-powerful

Omniscient: all-knowing

Jürgen Moltmann: *The Crucified God*

Jürgen Moltmann is a German theologian who, in his *The Crucified God* (1972) argued that God suffers with humanity. The following is a summary:

- The book is an attempt to answer Jesus' cry from the cross, 'My God, my God, why have you forsaken me?' Moltmann maintains that in the cross of Christ, God experienced death. The cross is therefore of great importance, not just for humankind, but for God.

- There is also an attempt to answer the question of what the cross means today. Moltmann argues that his theology of the cross is the reverse side of his theology of hope. Christian hope is based on the resurrection, but it cannot be a realistic and liberating hope 'unless it apprehends the pain of the negative'.

- Christian identity is 'an act of identification with the crucified Christ'. In him God has identified himself with those abandoned by God. Moltmann uses the story of a Jewish boy hanged by the Nazis in Auschwitz. God, he asserts, hung with him on the gallows, for God suffers with those who suffer.

- Therefore, Christian identification with the crucified Christ means solidarity with the poor, the oppressed and the alien. Its power is 'creative love (*agape*) for what is different, alien and ugly'.

- Many Christians do not truly understand what the cross symbolises. The church has made the cross attractive by stripping it of its true significance. For example, the Catholic concept of the mass as sacrifice denies the finality of Christ's death, which happened once and for all.

- In the Middle Ages the poor came to see the cross in a mystical way, in which God was recognised in the suffering Christ. This 'mysticism of the cross' is important because it shows God as suffering with the oppressed. This is meant to be the impetus for their liberation.

- Thus, following the crucified Christ 'is no longer a purely private and spiritualised matter, but develops into a political theology'.

- The meaning of Jesus' death cry, 'My God, my God, why have you forsaken me?' is that the 'abandonment on the cross ... is something which takes place within God himself ... The cross of the Son divides God from God to the utmost degree of enmity and distinction. The resurrection of the Son abandoned by God unites God with God in the most intimate fellowship'.

- Moltmann then asks: 'What does the cross of Jesus mean for God himself?'

- He answers that the crucified Jesus is God. God is not greater than he is in this humiliation ... not more glorious than he is in this self-surrender ... not more powerful than he is in this helplessness ... not more divine than he is in this humanity ... The Christ event on the cross is a God event.

- He then asserts that what he calls 'protest atheism' (i.e. atheism based on how the problem of evil and suffering destroys belief in a benevolent God) is resolved in the cross, where God himself protested against suffering in the death of the godforsaken Son.

- He dismisses as **docetism** the idea that it was only the human nature of Jesus that suffered while his divine nature of Jesus was unaffected.

- The cross is seen as the start of the divine process whereby the death of the Son and the grief of the Father led to the outpouring of the Holy Spirit.

Key person

Jürgen Moltmann (born 1926): an influential German theologian famous for his 'theology of hope', in which he asserts that God suffers with humanity and has promised humanity a better future based on the resurrection.

Jürgen Moltmann

Key term

Docetism: the heresy that Jesus did not suffer on the cross because his body was not human

Key quote

In the cross, Father and Son are most deeply separated in the forsakenness and at the same time are most inwardly one in their surrender. (Moltmann)

Key skills

Knowledge involves:

Selection of a range of (thorough) accurate and relevant information that is directly related to the specific demands of the question.

This means you choose the correct information relevant to the question set NOT the topic area. You will have to think and focus on selecting key information and NOT writing everything you know about the topic area.

Understanding involves:

Explanation that is extensive, demonstrating depth and/or breadth with excellent use of evidence and examples including (where appropriate) thorough and accurate supporting use of sacred texts, sources of wisdom and specialist language.

This means that you demonstrate that you understand something by being able to illustrate and expand your points through examples/supporting evidence in a personal way and NOT repeat chunks from a text book (known as rote learning).

Further application of skills:

Go through the topic areas in this section and create some bullet lists of key points from key areas. For each one, provide further elaboration and explanation through the use of evidence and examples.

AO1 Developing skills

It is now time to reflect upon the information that has been covered so far. It is also important to consider how what you have learned can be focused and used for examination-style answers by practising the skills associated with AO1.

Assessment objective 1 (AO1) involves demonstrating knowledge and understanding. The terms 'knowledge' and 'understanding' are obvious but it is crucial to be familiar with how certain skills demonstrate these terms, and also, how the performance of these skills is measured (see generic band descriptors Band 5 for AS AO1).

▶ **Your new task is this:** below is a weak answer that has been written in response to a question about why some theologians have expressed concern about the Bible's consistent use of male language about God. Using the band level descriptors you need to place this answer in a relevant band that corresponds to the description inside that band. It is obviously a weak answer and so would not be in bands 3–5. In order to do this it will be useful to consider what is missing from the answer and what is inaccurate. The accompanying analysis will assist you. In analysing the answer's weaknesses, in a group, think of five ways in which you would improve the answer in order to make it stronger. You may have more than five suggestions but try to negotiate as a group and prioritise the five most important things lacking.

Answer

The Bible speaks of God in terms of a human father and Jesus in terms of a human son [1]. The two, form a kind of divine boys' club [2]. The title 'Father' suggests several characteristics of God [3]. During his life on earth, Jesus was clearly a man. The Bible consistently refers to the Holy Spirit too in male terms [4]. Feminist theologians call this 'patriarchal language' [5]. It obscures the fact that God is in fact neither male nor female. As Jesus himself said, 'God is a spirit' [6].

Analysis of answer

1. No examples are given.
2. There is no mention of the third Person of the Trinity, the Holy Spirit.
3. The characteristics are not identified.
4. Some people see a correlation between the Holy Spirit and divine Wisdom, which is personified as a woman.
5. Define what is meant by 'patriarchal language'.
6. Where and when did he say this?

Issues for analysis and evaluation

The validity of referring to God as 'Mother'

The question depends on whether or not one considers the model of God as Father as adequate. Some Christians would say that it is. It conveys God's character and purpose for humankind. It describes one who creates or founds something. God is the creator of everything that has life. He is also the founder of truth and love. It expresses all the characteristics of a God who loves his children, rewards them when they seek him, communicates with them through his word and disciplines them when necessary. In the Bible God chose to reveal his identity in masculine language, which tells us something about his nature and character as creator, provider.

The main challenge to all this, however, is the question, 'Why are all such characteristics of God seen as belonging to the male gender?'

In addition, Jesus constantly referred to God as 'Abba', the affectionate term that children in Palestine would use for their father ('Daddy'). Paul writes that those who believe in Jesus can also now call God 'Abba' (Romans 8:15). They can have a personal relationship with God that goes beyond acknowledging him as creator.

Once again, the question emerges in response to this, 'Why cannot a Christian have a personal relationship with God as Mother and creator?'

There is a strong argument that the use of 'Father' should be seen in the patriarchal context and is not really a strong argument to use on its own because the Bible appears to have been written by men for men. Some would argue that God as Father is patriarchal language and shapes our image of God, which in turn shapes our relationship with God and other people. It could follow that if men think of God only in terms of 'fatherly' characteristics, such as power and authority, they are likely to exploit women and to abuse the earth.

Indeed, a further development of this argument would be that the Bible conveys a violent, militaristic, male God and has led to male domination of women. It ignores the biblical use of female images for God, e.g. the personification of God's Wisdom as a woman (Proverbs 8), and fails to convey the motherly, nurturing characteristics of God.

Moreover, the Father–Son bond between God and Jesus is a relationship that seems to exclude women and it must be remembered that God's nature has no gender, but it embodies feminine characteristics, such as compassion, grace, love, which are equally important as the masculine characteristics of redeeming, administering justice, and establishing peace.

In addition, the Bible contains several female images of God. In the Old Testament, Isaiah describes God as a comforting mother. In the New Testament, Jesus compares God to a woman searching for a lost coin. This image of God as sustainer and healer is not just scriptural: it is part of people's life experience.

However, in contrast to this, one argument that is often presented is that the concept of God as Mother of the world is suspect as it brings to mind ancient Near Eastern cults where the mother-goddess gives birth to the earth. Nonetheless, whilst this is an argument that clarifies why the Bible may have a male focus on God in its original context, this does not mean that this has to be the case today.

In conclusion, it is clear that the concept of God as Mother has been a cause of controversy for some, but has proved helpful to many Christians and is gaining increasing validity in Christian circles. There are arguments still presented against it; however, they are not necessarily strong enough to resist the challenge of God as Mother. Anyway, does it have to be one or the other or can we look forward to a day in which Christianity may embrace both understandings as useful for developing our understanding of the Christian God? For these reasons, the model of God as Father as the only model for Christians can be argued to be inadequate today, and it could be concluded that it is entirely valid to refer to God as Mother.

This section covers AO2 content and skills

Specification content

The validity of referring to God as 'Mother'.

AO2 Activity Possible lines of argument

Listed below are some conclusions that could be drawn from the AO2 reasoning in the above text:

1. The concept of God as Mother is unnecessary because the concept of God as Father is entirely adequate.

2. The concept of God as Mother is unbiblical.

3. The concept of God as Mother is necessary because it reflects other characteristics of God.

4. The concept of God as Mother is entirely biblical.

Consider each of the conclusions drawn above and collect evidence and examples to support each argument from the AO1 and AO2 material studied in this section. Select one conclusion that you think is most convincing and explain why it is so. Now contrast this with the weakest conclusion in the list, justifying your argument with clear reasoning and evidence.

The theological implications of a suffering God

Some people would argue that God cannot suffer. They would base their argument on the belief that impassibility is as much an attribute of God as his omniscience, his omnipotence, etc. God is above human suffering and emotion and, untouched by them.

Theologians who argue in favour of a passible God are accused of panentheism. They make God part of the natural world, infected with evil and suffering. If God is part of the natural world, he cannot be its omnipotent Creator. And if he is infected with evil, he can no longer be omnibenevolent.

Moreover, such arguments would suggest that if God can suffer, he loses his transcendence and cannot therefore free humankind from sin and death.

In addition, several of God's other essential attributes rule out any ability to suffer. His immutability means that he cannot respond to pain, as that would entail change. His omnipotence means that he is not subject to anything, including suffering.

However, there is an argument that contradicts this based upon biblical evidence. The Old Testament often refers to God responding to events on earth, sometimes with compassion, sometimes with anger. In the New Testament, Jesus (who is God) often shows his passibility, e.g. he feels pain at being rejected and weeps at the death of Lazarus. Jesus often displays emotions such as 'mercy' and also 'anger'.

However, in response to this, some argue that whilst God is able to feel emotion and pain, particularly through Jesus' passion and the cross, this does not, however, affect the impassibility of his divine nature, as Jesus is both fully human and fully divine. Yet it has always been God's plan to overcome the suffering with resurrection.

Others, like Moltmann, also disagree with the traditional ideas of the impassibility of God and aim to redefine or clarify them. They argue that in order to be omniscient, God must be able to experience suffering and emotions. As we have seen, Moltmann argues that his theology of the cross is the reverse side of his theology of hope. He argues that Christian hope is based on the resurrection, and as such it cannot be a realistic and liberating hope 'unless it apprehends the pain of the negative'.

It could be argued that to affirm the impassibility of God as an isolated concept is useful for theological purposes but seems to betray the biblical images of a God who is involved with his creation. It could be argued that it even demotes God to the 'Prime Mover' of Aristotle. To be engaged with, and yet remain separate from, creation is not a new idea. Muslims hold to the imminence/immanance of God and yet maintain Allah's transcendence.

In conclusion, God's divine sympathy means that he must be emotionally involved with his creation but maybe there is more to it than this, as we are assuming God has the same experience? While God is transcendent, he is not aloof. Also, the problem with the idea of passibility is the underlying assumption that our own understanding of our experiences of emotions equate to those of God. Surely God's emotions are consistent with God's perfect character and therefore not the same as our imperfect understanding and interpretation of them? In addition, the Oxford English Dictionary defines the word 'empathy' as 'the ability to understand and share the feelings of another'. Perhaps a way of maintaining the impassibility of the divine nature is to propose that Moltmann's God is 'empathetic', in that, whilst God understands and shares the suffering of others, God does not have ownership of the experience itself? This, then, could appease both traditional views of God's impassibility and those of theologians who have discussed this issue last century following the World Wars and the Holocaust.

AO2 Activity *Possible lines of argument*

Listed below are some conclusions that could be drawn from the AO2 reasoning in the above text:

1. An omnipotent, omniscient and immutable God cannot suffer.

2. In order to be omniscient, God must be able to experience suffering.

3. Jesus is God and Jesus certainly suffered.

Consider each of the conclusions drawn above and collect evidence and examples to support each argument from the AO1 and AO2 material studied in this section. Select one conclusion that you think is most convincing and explain why it is so. Now contrast this with the weakest conclusion in the list, justifying your argument with clear reasoning and evidence.

AO2 Developing skills

It is now time to reflect upon the information that has been covered so far. It is also important to consider how what you have learned can be focused and used for examination-style answers by practising the skills associated with AO2.

Assessment objective 2 (AO2) involves 'analysis' and 'evaluation'. The terms may be obvious but it is crucial to be familiar with how certain skills demonstrate these terms, and also, how the performance of these skills is measured (see generic band descriptors Band 5 for AS AO2).

Obviously, an answer is placed within an appropriate band descriptor depending upon how well the answer performs, ranging from excellent, good, satisfactory, basic/limited to very limited.

▶ **Your task is this:** below is a weak answer that has been written in response to a question requiring evaluation of the extent to which a suffering God is a contradiction in terms. Using the band level descriptors you need to place this answer in a relevant band that corresponds to the description inside that band. It is obviously a weak answer and so would not be in bands 3–5. In order to do this it will be useful to consider what is missing from the answer and what is inaccurate. The accompanying analysis will assist you. In analysing the answer's weaknesses, in a group, think of five ways in which you would improve the answer in order to make it stronger. You may have more than five suggestions but try to negotiate as a group and prioritise the five most important things lacking.

Key skills

Analysis involves identifying issues raised by the materials in the AO1, together with those identified in the AO2 section, and presents sustained and clear views, either of scholars or from a personal perspective ready for evaluation.

This means that it picks out key things to debate and the lines of argument presented by others or a personal point of view.

Evaluation involves considering the various implications of the issues raised based upon the evidence gleaned from analysis and provides an extensive detailed argument with a clear conclusion.

This means that the answer weighs up the various and different lines of argument analysed through individual commentary and response and arrives at a conclusion through a clear process of reasoning

Answer

Theologians who argue in favour of a passible [1] God are panentheists [2]. If God is just part of the natural world, he cannot be its Creator. And if he is infected with the evil of the world, he cannot be omnibenevolent. A passible God can suffer with all who suffer, but he can no longer free humankind from sin and death [3]. Stripped of his omnipotence and omnibenevolence, he is no more powerful than we are [4].

However, God is also said to be omniscient. He cannot be omniscient unless he is able to experience human emotions. In the Old Testament, God does not show any emotional involvement with his people [5], but in the Gospels, Jesus often shows his compassion [6] for suffering humanity [7].

Analysis of answer

1 What does the word *passible* mean?

2 What does the word *panentheist* mean?

3 Why? It needs to be explained that the panentheist God appears to have lost his transcendence.

4 What about the incarnation, when God became one of us?

5 This statement is inaccurate. There are many examples in the Old Testament of God reacting to events on earth with anger, compassion, etc.

6 No examples are given.

7 There is no reasoned conclusion.

Specification content

The need for the doctrine of the Trinity: the nature and identity of Christ (issues of divinity and pre-existence) and Christ's relationship with the Father (coequal and coeternal). The origin of the Holy Spirit: the *filioque* controversy.

Key terms

Adoptionism: the belief that Jesus was an ordinary man who became the Son of God only at his baptism

Arianism: the belief that Jesus was the highest of all created beings but not of the same substance as God

Sabellianism: the belief that Jesus was divine but not human

quickfire

2.6 What three heresies was the Nicene Creed of 325 CE designed to counteract?

Key quote

We worship one God in trinity and the Trinity in unity, neither confusing the persons nor dividing the divine being. For the Father is one person, the Son is another, and the Spirit is still another. But the deity of the Father, Son, and Holy Spirit is one, equal in glory, coeternal in majesty. (The Athanasian Creed)

B: The Trinity

The need for the doctrine of the Trinity

Christianity is a monotheistic religion. For most Christians, the Christian God exists as three Persons – Father (Creator), Son (Redeemer) and Holy Spirit (Sustainer). The doctrine of the Trinity was necessary to define the relationship between these three Persons.

The doctrine asserts three things:

1. The Father, Son, and Holy Spirit are three distinct Persons.
2. Each Person is fully God; the three are coexistent, coeternal and coequal.
3. There is only one God; the doctrine does not split God into three parts.

The belief is based on biblical testimony. It was Tertullian, in the 3rd century who coined the word 'Trinity' and the doctrine was formalised in the Nicene Creed (325 CE), which stated that the Son was 'of one substance' (Greek *homoousios*) with the Father.

The formula was designed to counteract what Tertullian saw as three contemporary heresies:

Adoptionism: the belief that Jesus was an ordinary man who became the Son of God only at his baptism.

Sabellianism: the belief that Jesus was divine but not human.

Arianism: the belief that Jesus was the highest of all created beings but not of the same substance as God.

One of the theologians present at the Council of Nicea in 325 CE was Athanasius. In the late 5th or early 6th century, his name was given to the Athanasian Creed, which is one of the best-known definitions of the Trinitarian doctrine.

The biblical foundations of the doctrine of the Trinity

The word 'Trinity' does not appear in the Bible, but some Christians argue that the concept that it represents – God as three coexistent, coeternal Persons – does.

In the Old Testament, God the Father is often referred to in the plural:

- The first Hebrew word used for God (Genesis 1:1) is *Elohim*, a plural noun (the singular is *El*). The same word is used many times throughout the Old Testament.
- In Genesis 1:26–27, God refers to himself in the plural: 'Let us make humankind in our image'.

In the New Testament, Jesus is often referred to as God:

- John 1 says that Jesus was the word and that word was God and that all things were created through him.
- In Philippians 2:10, Paul writes that Jesus, 'though he was in the form of God, did not regard equality with God as something to be exploited'.
- John 20:28 also states, 'My Lord and my God.'

The Holy Spirit too is referred to as God:

- In John 14:23 the indwelling of the Holy Spirit is linked to the indwelling of Jesus and his Father.
- In the Great Commission in Matthew 28:18–20, he sends the disciples to baptise all nations 'in the name of the Father and of the Son and of the Holy Spirit'.
- Paul, in Romans (8:11), tells his readers that if the Spirit of God (which he also calls 'the Spirit of Christ' (8:9)) dwells in them, God will give them life.

This famous icon of two angels visiting Abraham is interpreted by some as a foreshadowing of the doctrine of the Trinity

Study tip

Find more biblical evidence to support the doctrine of the Trinity and use this as evidence and examples in an answer.

The Bible teaches throughout that God is one.

- In the Old Testament, Deuteronomy 6:4–5 states unequivocally that God is one.
- In the New Testament, the statement is endorsed by Jesus in Mark 12:29 ('the Lord our God, the Lord is one') and by Paul in 1Corinthians 8:4 ('There is no God but one').

AO1 Activity

Design a flowchart highlighting the biblical references to the concept of the Trinity. This will help in selecting the key, relevant information for an answer to a question that expects a knowledge and understanding of the biblical foundations of the doctrine of the Trinity.

The Christian Church has never been able to explain adequately how God can be one, and at the same time three. It regards the Trinity as a mystery which reflects:

- that no human words can express the reality of God;
- that God is a community, a family of three in one.

Most Christians accept the Trinitarian formula, with the exception of a few denominations such as the Unitarian Church, which teach that Jesus was human and not God.

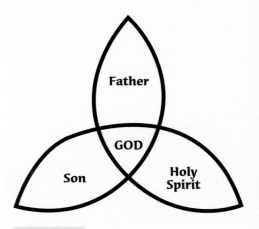

The Trinity

Key quote

The mystery of the Most Holy Trinity is the central mystery of Christian faith and life. It is the mystery of God in himself. (The Catechism of the Catholic Church)

Key term

Filioque: Latin for 'and the Son'

quickfire

2.7 What does the Latin word *filioque* mean?

Key quotes

… the Holy Spirit … proceeds from the Father. (Nicene Creed, Constantinople, 381 CE)

… the Holy Spirit … proceeds from the Father and the Son. (Nicene Creed Toledo, 589 CE)

Key idea 💡

The Filioque Controversy was to do with the origin of the Holy Spirit and specifically the Latin phrase, translated 'and the son', which was accepted as an addition to the Nicene Creed confirmed by the First Council of Constantinople in 381. The addition was included after the Synod of Toledo in Spain in 589 so it read: 'We believe in the Holy Spirit, the Lord, the giver of life, who proceeds from the Father **and the Son**. Who with the Father and the Son is worshipped and glorified.

The Filioque Controversy

You will recall that the doctrine of the Trinity was first formalised in the Christian creed agreed at the Council of Nicea in 325 CE. The creed states simply that Christians believe 'in the Holy Spirit'. There is no elaboration.

At the Council of Constantinople in 381 CE, the Nicene Creed was amended to contain the following words: '[We believe] in the Holy Spirit, the Lord, the Giver of Life, *who proceeds from the Father*'. All the churches represented at the Council had agreed to the new wording.

In 589 CE, at the Council of Toledo, however, there was another change. The clause about the Holy Spirit now reads: 'We believe in the Holy Spirit, the Lord, the Giver of Life, *who proceeds from the Father **and the Son***'. The three English words 'and the Son' are one word in Latin – *filioque*. Its inclusion in the Nicene Creed caused a controversy – the *Filioque* Controversy, which has lasted to this day.

It appears to have been added to reflect the thinking of several influential theologians in the 4th and 5th centuries including Hilary of Poitiers, Augustine of Hippo and Cyril of Alexandria, all of whom had written of the Holy Spirit proceeding 'from the Father and the Son'. The idea had become widely accepted in the Latin-speaking west, but not in the Greek-speaking east.

The word was added without the agreement of the five patriarchs of the church (the patriarchs of Jerusalem, Antioch, Alexandria, Rome and Constantinople).

The dispute over *filioque* lasted for six centuries, but did not of itself divide the church. In 1014 CE, however, Pope Benedict VIII agreed to use the word for the first time at a Mass in Rome. Forty years later, Rome accused the Eastern Church of heresy for not accepting *filioque*. This charge, together with many other issues largely based on misunderstandings between the Greek and Latin traditions, and the east's opposition to the Pope making any change in the Nicene Creed without the agreement of an Ecumenical Council, led to the Great Schism of 1054 CE, which divided the Eastern and Western church and has continued to this day.

The Immanent Trinity and the Economic Trinity

- The term **Immanent Trinity** signifies what God *is* (i.e. three Persons, one God).
- The term **Economic Trinity** signifies what God *does* (i.e. the Father creates; the Son redeems; the Holy Spirit sanctifies).

The Council of Nicea (325 CE)

CONCILIVM NICAENVM·I

The Western Church accepted Augustine's argument that human beings can know the Trinity from their own experience because there are traces of the Trinity in the human soul (e.g. a triad of self-knowledge: memory, understanding, will). Augustine does not differentiate between the Immanent and the Economic Trinity.

For him, since the Holy Spirit acts within the Trinity as the bond of love between Father and Son, it follows that the Holy Spirit must proceed from both. And since the Holy Spirit acts within human beings to unite them too with the Father and the Son, and with each other, in this bond of love, it follows that human beings can derive the nature of God from this experience.

For the Eastern Church, however, Augustine's argument was unacceptable because human beings cannot base the doctrine of the Trinity on their own experience. That confuses the incomprehensible **structure** of the Trinity (three Persons, one God) with its **actions** (what the Trinity does in creation, e.g. the Holy Spirit uniting human beings in the Father–Son bond of love). It also makes the nature of God dependent upon created beings. The Immanent Trinity is therefore not the same as the Economic Trinity.

The Eastern Church accepts that the structure of God is a Trinity of three equal Persons, but does not accept that anything has been revealed to us of the inner being of God except that:

- the Father alone is the source of divinity;
- the Son alone is 'begotten' of the Father;
- the Spirit 'proceeds' from the Father alone.

AO1 Activity

Form two groups and imagine that you are debating the *filioque* issue in one of the early Christian councils. One group will prepare a one-minute speech in favour of *filioque*; the other group will prepare a one-minute speech against. Choose a member of each group to put your case to the whole class, and then decide who offered the better argument.

Modern developments of the Trinity

Despite its central importance in theological debate during the first ten centuries of the Christian Church, the doctrine of the Trinity was sidelined by succeeding generations. **Enlightenment** theologians found it problematic, as did Friedrich Schleiermacher (1768–1834), who tried to reconcile Enlightenment theology with traditional Christian beliefs. Schleiermacher dismissed the Trinity in a 14-page appendix to his 800-page theological work, *The Christian Faith* (1821).

A more recent development of the doctrine of the Trinity was produced by Karl Barth. In response to Schleiermacher, Barth placed a section on the Trinity at the beginning of his 14-volume *Church Dogmatics*, published between 1932 and 1967, to underline its central importance in Christian theology. 'The doctrine of the Trinity,' Barth wrote, 'is what basically distinguishes the Christian doctrine of God as Christian'.

For Barth, the basis of the doctrine of the Trinity is that God has revealed himself to human beings. This he has done in two movements:

1. In the Son: this is an objective 'unveiling' of what God is.
2. In the Spirit: this is a subjective reception, or 'imparting'; 'God working for us'.

quickfire

2.8 Define the terms *Immanent Trinity* and *Economic Trinity*.

Key person

Augustine of Hippo (354–430 CE): 5th-century scholar and bishop; one of the most important figures in early western Christianity.

Augustine of Hippo

Key term

The Enlightenment: an 18th-century philosophical movement based on reason, tolerance, liberty, etc.

Karl Barth

Key person

Karl Barth (1886–1968): a Swiss theologian whose work had a deep influence on 20th-century theology.

quickfire

2.9 According to Barth, what makes human beings respond to the revelation of God in Jesus?

Key terms

Logos asarkos: Greek for 'the Word without flesh'; Barth's term for the Son before he became incarnate

Objective: factual; not based on personal belief

Seinsweise: Barth's word for 'mode of being', which he uses instead of the usual word Person to refer to the three members of the Godhead

Subjective: personal belief; not based on facts

quickfire

2.10 What does the term *Seinsweise* signify in Barth's theology?

The **objective** unveiling of God in Jesus is not enough. There must also be a **subjective** recognition imparted by the Spirit. Barth illustrates this by imagining two men witnessing Jesus' crucifixion.

The first says, 'There is a common criminal being executed'. This man has not recognised the unveiling of God in Jesus.

The second man says, 'There is the Son of God dying for me'. To this man, the Holy Spirit has imparted the recognition of God in Jesus.

Barth concludes that human beings are incapable of responding to the objective revelation of God in Jesus, unless a recognition of that revelation is imparted to them by the Holy Spirit. This imparting by the Spirit proceeds from both the hidden Father and the revealed Son. Barth therefore endorses the use of the word *filioque*. The imparting is done through God's grace. Grace, or 'good favour', is an attribute of God. But grace also is 'the Holy Spirit received'.

The imparting therefore is not simply God's action through the Spirit. It reflects also the Father's grace, which is a true 'mode of being' within God himself.

Thus, for Barth, as for Augustine, the Immanent Trinity (who God is) is reflected in the Economic Trinity (God working for us).

Study tip

Make sure that you are familiar with all the key terms and their correct definitions. This is especially relevant for this section. This will ensure that you are making 'thorough and accurate use of specialist language and vocabulary in context' (L5 band descriptor AO1).

Problems with modern developments of the Trinity

Barth's model of the Trinity has been criticised on several grounds:

- For the Eastern Orthodox Church, its merging of the Immanent Trinity and the Economic Trinity and its endorsement of the *filioque* clause make it a heresy.
- Western theologians, including Jürgen Moltmann, have complained that its use of the term **Seinsweise** ('mode of being'), instead of the usual term 'Person' to refer to the members of the Godhead brings to mind the heresy of Modalism. Modalism teaches that God is a single Person who, throughout history, has revealed himself in three different modes: Father (before the Incarnation), Son (in Jesus), Holy Spirit (after Jesus' ascension).
- It does not distinguish between the Father, the Son and the Holy Spirit.
- It sees the Father, Son and Holy Spirit as one God in eternal repetition. This must mean that the Father, Son and Holy Spirit exist one after the other, never at the same time. This destroys the eternal unity of the Godhead.

These criticisms have been answered as follows:

- The Western Church has for centuries accepted the merging of the Immanent Trinity and the Economic Trinity and the *filioque* clause.
- While it is true that Barth uses the term 'modes of being' (*Seinsweise*) instead of 'Persons' for the three members of the Trinity, he does so in order to avoid confusing the word 'person' with 'personality'. To say that God has three 'personalities' is Tritheism. Barth writes: 'the one personal God is what He is not just in one mode … but in the mode of the Father, in the mode of the Son, and in the mode of the Holy Spirit'. There are three modes, but one personality. Barth does, however, distinguish between the three modes; e.g. although the incarnation is a work of the entire Trinity, it is the mode of the Son – not the Father, not the Holy Spirit – who becomes flesh.

- Barth distinguishes the Father from the Son by his use of the Greek term *Logos asarkos* for the Son. *Logos asarkos* means 'the Word without flesh', i.e. God the Son as he lived in the Godhead, distinct from God the Father, before the incarnation. Here Barth makes a distinction between the Son of God and the Son of Man. While the Son of God is the title for the eternal Word, the Son of Man is the title for Jesus incarnated. Thus, while the three modes of being in the Godhead exist in perfect unity, the second mode (the Son) has a distinct place, and becomes Jesus of Nazareth. Barth then makes a distinction between Jesus and the Holy Spirit. It is the Holy Spirit that bears witness to the work of the Son.

- While it is true that he sees the Father, Son and Holy Spirit as 'one God in threefold repetition', Barth insists that 'He is the one God in each repetition'. The aim is to highlight the unchanging nature of the one eternal Trinity.

- God is 'unimpaired unity', but also 'unimpaired distinction' as Revealer (Father), Revelation (Son), Revealedness (Spirit).

AO1 Activity

Above is a summary of some key problems with the modern developments of the Trinity. Obviously you could not cover them all in an answer, so select three or four that you would use to write about the Trinity bearing in mind the three elements of the Specification: 'nature and identity of Christ'; 'relationship with the Father'; and, 'the origin of the Holy Spirit.'

Study tip

Make sure that you always answer the question set, paying particular attention to key words. This will ensure that you have the best chance of giving 'an extensive and relevant response which answers the specific demands of the question set' (L5 band descriptor AO1).

Meister Francke: Man of Sorrows with Angels

Key quote

In the beginning was the Word, and the Word was with God, and the Word was God. He was with God in the beginning. Through him all things were made; without him nothing was made that has been made. In him was life, and that life was the light of all mankind. The light shines in the darkness, and the darkness has not overcome it. (John 1:1–5)

Key quote

The Word became flesh and made his dwelling among us. We have seen his glory, the glory of the one and only Son, who came from the Father, full of grace and truth. (John 1:14)

Key skills

Knowledge involves:

Selection of a range of (thorough) accurate and relevant information that is directly related to the specific demands of the question.

This means you choose the correct information relevant to the question set NOT the topic area. You will have to think and focus on selecting key information and NOT writing everything you know about the topic area.

Understanding involves:

Explanation that is extensive, demonstrating depth and/or breadth with excellent use of evidence and examples including (where appropriate) thorough and accurate supporting use of sacred texts, sources of wisdom and specialist language.

This means that you demonstrate that you understand something by being able to illustrate and expand your points through examples/supporting evidence in a personal way and NOT repeat chunks from a text book (known as rote learning).

Further application of skills:

Go through the topic areas in this section and create some bullet lists of key points from key areas. For each one, provide further elaboration and explanation through the use of evidence and examples.

Analysis of answer

1. Where does he do this, and why was the development necessary?

2. What else in Barth's model goes against the teaching of the Eastern Church?

3. Examples?

4. What was Barth's defence of his use of the word *Seinsweise* against the accusation of modalism?

5. What does the term *Logos asarkos* mean?

AO1 Developing skills

It is now time to reflect upon the information that has been covered so far. It is also important to consider how what you have learned can be focused and used for examination-style answers by practising the skills associated with AO1.

Assessment objective 1 (AO1) involves demonstrating knowledge and understanding. The terms 'knowledge' and 'understanding' are obvious but it is crucial to be familiar with how certain skills demonstrate these terms, and also, how the performance of these skills is measured (see generic band descriptors Band 5 for AS AO1).

▶ **Your new task is this:** below is a fairly strong answer, although not perfect, that has been written in response to a question requiring an examination of modern developments of the Trinity. Using the band level descriptors you can compare this with the relevant higher bands and the descriptions inside those bands. It is obviously a fairly strong answer and so would not be in bands 5, 1or 2. In order to do this it will be useful to consider what is both strong and weak about the answer and therefore what needs developing. The accompanying comments will assist you, but they are incomplete.

In analysing the answer, in a group, identify three ways to make this answer a better one. You may have more than three observations and indeed suggestions to make it a perfect answer!

Answer

In the mid 20th century Karl Barth, a Swiss theologian, developed the concept of the doctrine of the Trinity [1]. It is, he wrote, 'what basically distinguishes the Christian doctrine of God as Christian'.

For Barth, the basis of the doctrine is that God has revealed himself to human beings. First, he revealed himself objectively in the Son. Second, he reveals himself subjectively in the Holy Spirit. The first revelation is incomplete without the other. Without the Holy Spirit, people cannot recognise Jesus as the Son of God.

The Spirit proceeds from both the Father and the Son – *filioque*. The imparting of the Spirit is done through God's grace. Grace is an attribute of God. It is a true 'mode of being' within God himself. Barth's word for 'mode of being' is *Seinsweise*.

The endorsement of *filioque* obviously makes Barth's model a heresy for Eastern theologians [2].

Western theologians [3], have criticised his use of the term *Seinsweise,* instead of the usual term 'Person' for members of the Godhead. This, they say, smacks of Modalism, a heresy teaching that God has revealed himself in three different modes at different times: Father (before Jesus), Son (in Jesus), Holy Spirit (after Jesus). If Father, Son and Holy Spirit exist consecutively, they cannot be One [4].

The Modalist heresy is also accused of failing to distinguish between the three Persons of the Trinity. The Son and the Spirit are simply 'manifestations' of the One God. Barth, however, distinguishes the Father from the Son by his use of the Greek term *Logos asarkos* for the Son before the incarnation [5]. While Father, Son and Holy Spirit exist in perfect unity, the Son has a distinct place, and becomes Jesus of Nazareth. The Holy Spirit then bears witness to the Son's work.

Issues for analysis and evaluation

The monotheistic claims of the doctrine of the Trinity

The area of contention here is that to conceptually speak of three in one is a logical nonsense. However, the debate surrounding the Trinity attempts to clarify the confusion and claim that this is a misapprehension in that whilst we speak of three in one, the three is only a matter of theological differentiation in purpose, and not in identity.

Jews and Muslims often comment that the doctrine of the Trinity suggests that there are three separate Christian Gods. The idea of separate aspects of a universal deity, is, however, not new. Indeed, it is consistent with the Hindu concept of Brahman (the One true ultimate Spirit) and the many incarnations of Brahman through countless deities or avatars.

Others argue that Father, Son and Holy Spirit are analogous to the finite gods of ancient pagan religions. This, however, is strongly rejected as a very simplistic view of the Trinity. Nonetheless, there are some Christian denominations (e.g. the Unitarian Church) who would agree, arguing that the Son and the Spirit are not God.

Another argument related to this is that even if the Son was God, for the three decades that he lived on earth, he and the Father must have been two separate beings.

Some would argue that the Christian Church has never been able to give an adequate explanation or to provide an adequate analogy of the Trinity. However, many Christian denominations insist that God is 'triune', that is, that God is one, but exists in three Persons. If the doctrine were polytheistic, Father, Son and Holy Spirit would have to be three separate gods and this is definitely seen to be heresy. Christianity is monotheistic.

Some analogies are seen as tolerable attempts at explaining the doctrine. Augustine compared the Trinity to the three parts of a human being: mind, spirit, and will. They are three distinct but inseparable aspects, and together constitute one unified human being.

An anonymous medieval Welsh theologian drew an analogy between the Trinity and the capital letter A. The letter A consists of three lines. Each line needs the others to exist as a letter. If we give each line a name (Father, Son and Holy Spirit), we have a material example of the Trinity.

Mainstream Christianity thinks it a heresy (Arianism) to argue that the Son was not God.

The Bible maintains that God is love. Love can exist only in a relationship. The Trinity is a relationship of love. The Father loves the Son and the Son loves the Father. The Holy Spirit is the love that they exchange, and have gifted to humankind so that they too may be brought into the Trinitarian relationship.

In conclusion, it can be seen that the doctrine of the Trinity has caused confusion, argument and misunderstanding both within Christianity and beyond. On the one level there could be argued to be a logical inconsistency, and affirmers of the Trinity propose that this is due to an inherent misconception that the 'three' is referring to separate 'being' when speaking of the Immanent Trinity. Whilst many have tried to justify this logical inconsistency through an explanation of the Economic Trinity, questions still remain. Perhaps, just as the creation of the world, the resurrection of Jesus and the doctrine of incarnation are seen as divine mysteries and a matter of faith, maybe the best solution would be to locate a belief in the Trinity within the parameters of faith as opposed to being determined by reason?

This section covers AO2 content and skills

Specification content
The monotheistic claims of the doctrine of the Trinity.

AO2 Activity *Possible lines of argument*

Listed below are some conclusions that could be drawn from the AO2 reasoning in the above text:

1. The doctrine of the Trinity makes Christianity a polytheistic religion.

2. The doctrine of the Trinity preserves Christianity's alleged monotheism.

3. The doctrine of the Trinity defies logic.

4. The doctrine of the Trinity demonstrates that God is love.

Consider each of the conclusions drawn above and collect evidence and examples to support each argument from the AO1 and AO2 material studied in this section. Select one conclusion that you think is most convincing and explain why it is so. Now contrast this with the weakest conclusion in the list, justifying your argument with clear reasoning and evidence.

Specification content

Whether the doctrine of the Trinity is necessary to understand the God of Christianity.

Whether the doctrine of the Trinity is necessary to understand the God of Christianity

Some people dismiss the doctrine of the Trinity as merely an abstract belief that makes no logical sense. The English theologian Karen Kilby has written that 'the doctrine of the Trinity so easily appears to be an intellectual puzzle with no relevance to the faith of most Christians'.

Far from helping to understand Christianity, the Trinitarian idea has confused things, giving rise to several theories considered so misleading that they were declared heresies. Among these heresies were Modalism (the idea that the one God reveals himself in different ways at different times, sometimes as Father, sometimes as Son, sometimes as Holy Spirit); Tritheism (the idea that Father, Son and Holy Spirit are three separate gods); Adoptionism (the idea that Jesus was born human and only adopted as God's Son at his baptism or resurrection); and Arianism (the belief that Jesus was the highest of all created beings but not of the same substance as God).

The disagreement over the addition of the word *filioque* to the Nicene Creed led to the Great Schism of 1054, from which the Christian Church has never recovered. While both churches had originally believed that the Holy Spirit proceeded only from the Father, the Western Church came to believe that the Holy Spirit proceeded from both the Father 'and the Son' (*filioque*). The Eastern Church excommunicated the Western Church for unilaterally introducing such a major change to Christian belief.

Others would say that the doctrine of the Trinity is fundamental to the understanding of Christianity.

First of all, it interprets monotheism in the light of of a specific set of events and experiences revealed in the Christian scriptures. It is the only way in which Christians can make sense of the content and teaching of the Bible. It states that God must be simultaneously both Three and One. This is a central element of Christian identity.

Second, it is not just an abstract belief. It plays a central part in the worship of all mainstream Christian traditions. For example, baptism is carried out and blessings are given 'In the name of the Father and of the Son and of the Holy Spirit'; Christian creeds, Eucharistic prayers, doxologies and many hymns are firmly Trinitarian. Christians understand that they must worship God the Father; follow the example set by God the Son and that God the Holy Spirit lives in them.

Third, while it teaches that God is a mystery that human thought cannot fully comprehend, it nevertheless sees God as a community of three Persons coexisting in a coequal relationship of eternal love. This provides a model for human relationships, as individuals, families and as a community.

In conclusion, whatever position is taken with regard to the meaning, interpretation and understanding of the doctrine of Trinity in Christianity, the debate does suggest the possibility that there can be no absolutely coherent and universal agreement. Therefore, to suggest that an understanding of the doctrine of the Trinity is necessary to understand the God of Christianity all depends upon what 'understanding' pertains to. Perhaps the Bible contains the answer as to what is necessary to know about the Christian God when it states in 1 John 4:8: 'whoever does not love does not know God, because God is love' and also again in 4:12 that 'No one has ever seen God; but if we love one another, God lives in us and his love is made complete in us'.

AO2 Activity Possible lines of argument

Listed below are some conclusions that could be drawn from the AO2 reasoning in the above text:

1. The doctrine of the Trinity is essential to our understanding of the God of Christianity.

2. The doctrine of the Trinity enhances our understanding of the God of Christianity.

3. The doctrine of the Trinity confuses our understanding of the God of Christianity.

4. The doctrine of the Trinity is irrelevant to our understanding of the God of Christianity.

Consider each of the conclusions drawn above and collect evidence and examples to support each argument from the AO1 and AO2 material studied in this section. Select one conclusion that you think is most convincing and explain why it is so. Now contrast this with the weakest conclusion in the list, justifying your argument with clear reasoning and evidence.

AO2 Developing skills

It is now time to reflect upon the information that has been covered so far. It is also important to consider how what you have learned can be focused and used for examination-style answers by practising the skills associated with AO2.

Assessment objective 2 (AO2) involves 'analysis' and 'evaluation'. The terms may be obvious but it is crucial to be familiar with how certain skills demonstrate these terms, and also, how the performance of these skills is measured (see generic band descriptors Band 5 for AS AO2).

Obviously an answer is placed within an appropriate band descriptor depending upon how well the answer performs, ranging from excellent, good, satisfactory, basic/limited to very limited.

▶ **Your task is this:** below is a reasonable answer, although not perfect, that has been written in response to a question requiring an examination of whether or not the doctrine of the Trinity is unbiblical. Using the band level descriptors you can compare this with the relevant higher bands and the descriptions inside those bands. It is obviously a reasonable answer and so would not be in bands 5, 1 or 2. In order to do this it will be useful to consider what is both strong and weak about the answer and therefore what needs developing.

In analysing the answer, in a group, identify three ways to make this answer a better one. You may have more than three observations and indeed suggestions to make it a perfect answer!

Key skills

Analysis involves identifying issues raised by the materials in the AO1, together with those identified in the AO2 section, and presents sustained and clear views, either of scholars or from a personal perspective ready for evaluation.

This means that it picks out key things to debate and the lines of argument presented by others or a personal point of view.

Evaluation involves considering the various implications of the issues raised based upon the evidence gleaned from analysis and provides an extensive detailed argument with a clear conclusion.

This means that the answer weighs up the various and different lines of argument analysed through individual commentary and response and arrives at a conclusion through a clear process of reasoning.

Answer

The word 'Trinity' does not appear in the Bible and the Trinitarian doctrine is not set out in a single biblical verse or passage. On the contrary, the Bible insists that there is only one God. The Old Testament has no awareness of a Trinity, and neither, apparently does Jesus in his teaching.

In the Old Testament, the Book of Deuteronomy states unequivocally that 'the Lord our God, the Lord is one', and this is endorsed in the New Testament both by Jesus and by Paul. In the Gospel of John, Jesus calls God the Father 'the only true God'. This cannot be the case if Jesus and the Holy Spirit also claim to be God. Jesus also tells his disciples in John that he is going to the Father, 'because the Father is greater than I'.

On the other hand, it is true that in the New Testament Jesus is often referred to as God. John 1 says that Jesus was the Word and the Word was God and that all things were created through him. In Philippians 2, Paul writes that Jesus, 'though he was in the form of God, did not regard equality with God as something to be exploited'.

The Holy Spirit too is referred to as God. In John 14, Jesus speaks of the Holy Spirit as equal with himself and the Father. In the Great Commission in Matthew 28, he sends the disciples to baptise all nations 'in the name of the Father and of the Son and of the Holy Spirit'. Paul, in his Letter to the Romans, tells his readers that if the Spirit of God dwells in them, God will give them life.

The Old Testament is therefore clear that God the Father is the only one God. However, the New Testament, with its references not only to Jesus as God's Son but also to the Holy Spirit as the Spirit of God, seems to suggest that God is Triune, consisting of three Persons, Father, Son and Holy Spirit. It thus became necessary to formulate the doctrine of the Trinity to explain the relationship between the three.

Specification content

Three theories of the atonement (which are not mutually exclusive): the death of Jesus as Christus Victor (with reference to the liberation of humanity from hostile powers); the death of Jesus as a substitution (both the belief that Jesus died as a substitute for humanity, and the belief that only the divine-human Jesus could act as a sacrifice by God for the sake of humanity); the death of Jesus as a moral example (of how to live and die). The underlying assumptions about the need for divine forgiveness and the conflict between the wrath and love of God in theories of the atonement.

quickfire

2.11 What is meant by *original sin*?

quickfire

2.12 What is the meaning of *atonement*?

Key terms

Atonement: to make 'at one' or reconcile

Expiation: what Christ did on the cross – he paid the penalty for human sin

Propitiation: the result of what Christ did on the cross – he averted God's wrath

quickfire

2.13 What is the difference between *expiation* and *propitiation*?

C: The atonement

The atonement: definition

Most religions have rituals, often involving sacrifice, by which people are reconciled with the deity. In Christianity, **atonement** is the process by which men and women are reconciled with God through the death of Jesus on the cross.

Reconciliation was necessary because all people had sinned. Genesis 3 tells how sin first came into the world when the devil successfully tempted the first man and woman, Adam and Eve. Christianity teaches that we all carry this sin within us. It is called 'original sin', and it separates us from God. Thus, God and humankind need to be reconciled.

The word 'atonement' has been used in the English language since the 16th century to convey the significance of Jesus' death. It was coined from the two words 'at one' by William Tyndale (1494–1536), one of the first translators of the Bible into English. 'At-one-ment' simply means 'to set at one' or 'to reconcile'. Whereas the older English versions of the Bible , including the King James Version of 1611, use the word to translate the Hebrew *kippûr* and the Greek *katallage*, most modern versions use the word 'reconciliation'.

The New Testament uses several different models to convey how God reconciled humankind to himself through Jesus' death. One model is Jesus as 'the Lamb of God who takes away the sin of the world'; another is the payment of a ransom to free a slave; another is a military victory. But there is no single doctrine of atonement, nor does the Christian Church have a single definition of what the death of Jesus means.

There are, however, a number of theories. Most of them make use of two technical terms, **expiation** and **propitiation**. *Expiation* means 'removing guilt by paying a penalty'. *Propitiation* means 'turning away wrath by making an offering'.

Early models (sacrifice and ransom)

In the Old Testament, sacrifice was a common practice aimed at restoring a broken relationship between people and God. Leviticus 16:20–22 describes a process by which the priest symbolically lays the sins of the community upon a goat, which is then cast out into the wilderness. Exodus 12:24–27 commands the Jews to slaughter and eat a lamb on the first night of the feast of Passover to remember their deliverance from Egypt. When John the Baptist said of Jesus that he was 'the Lamb of God who takes away the sin of the world' (John 1:29), the idea would have been familiar to his listeners.

Holman Hunt: The Scapegoat

The Epistle to the Hebrews is the most extensive New Testament treatment of Jesus' death as a sacrifice. It states that through the perfect sacrifice of Jesus, human sin was taken away 'once for all' (Hebrews 7:27). Jesus' death on the cross was thus a complete expiation, a final atonement for sin.

Study tip

Find out more about the Jewish concept of the Passover lamb.

Early Christian theologians took up the image. Asserting that human beings had nothing of sufficient value to sacrifice to God for their sins, they argued that God himself had provided the sacrifice for them, as he did in the story of Abraham and Isaac (Genesis 22:8). Augustine wrote in *The City of God* about 420 CE: '[Jesus] offered sacrifice for our sins. And where did he find that offering, the pure victim that he would offer? He offered himself.'

Many people have, of course, objected to this model on the grounds that no loving God would offer his only Son as a sacrifice in order to satisfy his own sense of justice. If that were true, they argue, then the Christian God is an angry tyrant who must be appeased before he forgives.

A variant of the Sacrificial model of the atonement is the Ransom model. The Gospels indicate that Jesus himself thought of his death in terms of a ransom payment to redeem men and women from sin. Matthew 20:28 quotes him as saying that 'the Son of Man came ... to give his life a ransom for many'. The idea is repeated elsewhere in the New Testament, e.g. in I Timothy 2:5–6, Paul speaks of 'Jesus... who gave himself a ransom for all'.

It is not clear, however, to whom the ransom was paid. Origen, a 2nd-century theologian, maintained that Jesus' death was a ransom payment to Satan, to free humankind whom Satan had enslaved following Adam and Eve's sin. As Satan was unaware that Jesus was God, he was deceived. He then suffered a final defeat when Jesus was resurrected.

Study tip

When you use references to scholars and texts, or direct quotations from theologians, try to make them manageable in size. Sometimes extracts are just as effective. In addition, do not just write down a quote to 'show off' without thinking about how it fits in with the point you are making.

Many people have objected to this model on the grounds that it gives Satan more power than he has and that it makes God both a debtor and a deceiver.

Christus Victor

In 1931, the Swedish theologian Gustaf Aulén, repopularised the Ransom model in his influential book, *Christus Victor*, in which he argued that human beings had indeed been bound by the hostile powers of death and the devil. According to Aulén, however, the Ransom model is not a theological hypothesis but a passion story about God conquering these powers and thus liberating his people from the bondage of sin and death. In Aulén's words, 'the work of Christ is first and foremost a victory over the powers that hold mankind in bondage: sin, death, and the devil'.

Thus, whereas Anselm saw the atonement as the payment of a debt of honour to God, Aulén sees it in terms of human beings being liberated from the slavery of sin, of Jesus by his incarnation entering human misery and redeeming it.

Key quote

[The priest] shall lay both hands on the head of the live goat and confess over it all the iniquities of the people of Israel ... The goat shall bear on itself all their iniquities to a barren region; and the goat shall be set free in the wilderness. (Leviticus 16:21–22)

Key quote

The payment could not be made to God, because God was not holding sinners in captivity for a ransom, so the payment had to be to the devil. (Origen)

Key quote

Through a tree we were made debtors to God; so through a tree we have our debt cancelled.

(Irenaeus)

The *Christus Victor* model has been criticised on the grounds that it plays down human sin and guilt and is comfortably triumphalist. It is, however, similar in many respects to Irenaeus' Recapitulation model, in which the 2nd-century Irenaeus modified the Ransom model of atonement, arguing that God was no debtor to Satan but that human beings, having fallen prey to Satan's seduction in the Fall, were debtors to God. Their debt was cancelled when Jesus 'waged war' against the devil, 'and crushed him who had at the beginning led us captives in Adam'. Jesus 'became what we are that we could become what he is'. This is still the favoured view of the Eastern Orthodox Church.

Gustaf Aulén on the right

The Cross as Satisfaction and Penal Substitution

Satisfaction

In this context, the word 'satisfaction' does not mean 'fulfilment' or 'pleasure'. It means 'reparation', 'recompense', 'propitiation'.

In his book, *Cur Deus Homo* (1097), Anselm, who was Archbishop of Canterbury from 1093 to 1109, proposed the Satisfaction model of the atonement, a modification of the Ransom model. Anselm maintained that human sin had so offended God's honour that he could only be satisfied by the death of the God-man, Jesus.

Anselm believed that the human debt to God was greater than men and women were able to pay. Therefore, God had to pay the debt himself. But the payment would not redeem human beings unless it was made by a human. God therefore became a human being in Jesus so that he could pay the debt to himself.

Jesus was under no obligation to die, but his death brought infinite honour to God and gained Jesus a 'superabundance' or '**supererogation**' of merit. The reward (reconciliation with God), of which of course Jesus himself had no need, as he was sinless, he passed on to those who believed in him.

Anselm's Satisfaction model has been criticised on the grounds that it was based on the concept of 'honour', a central concept in the feudal system of his day, in which serfs were bound to an overlord who in turn was bound to the king. Serfs owed their overlord a debt of honour for protecting them, as did the overlord to the king. Anselm saw God in these terms – as the overlord of the world. Therefore, it is criticised for depending too much on an unbiblical model.

St Anselm

Key person

Anselm (c.1033–1109): Italian born monk and theologian, appointed Archbishop of Canterbury by William II.

Key term

Supererogation: doing more than duty requires

Penal substitution

The 16th-century Protestant reformers considered Anselm's Satisfaction model inadequate because it was based on the concept of God's honour rather than on that of God's justice. They proposed an alternative Penal Substitution model: that Jesus set human beings free from being punished for their sins by taking that punishment upon himself on the cross, thus satisfying the justice of God.

They based their argument on the Suffering Servant Songs in the Old Testament Book of Isaiah, where there are famous descriptions of vicarious suffering; for example, 'the Lord has laid on him the iniquity of us all' (Isaiah 53:6), and some passages in Paul's Epistles; for example, ' Christ redeemed us from the curse of the law by becoming a curse for us' (Galatians 3:13).

The Penal Substitution model has been criticised on the grounds that:

- It is based more on a criminal justice system than on biblical revelation.
- No criminal justice system would justify punishing the innocent instead of the guilty.
- It is a model rooted in violence. It portrays God too much as a God of vengeance who insists that his own son suffers spiritually and physically.
- It separates the Father and the Son. It is as if the Son saves us from the Father.
- It is incompatible with any proper Christian understanding of the nature of God.

The crucifixion of Jesus

Key quote

What sort of God was this, getting so angry with the world and the people he created and then, to calm himself down, demanding the blood of his own son? … And anyway, why should God forgive us through punishing somebody else? It was worse than illogical, it was insane. It made God sound like a psychopath. If any human being behaved like this, we would say they were a monster. (Jeffrey John, Dean of St Albans)

Key quote

Christ redeemed us from the curse of the law by becoming a curse for us. (Galatians 3:13)

Others have argued that the Penal Substitution model is the mechanism by which everything else achieved by Jesus on the cross:

- *The cross as ransom*: the image works only if Jesus took our punishment. *The cross as example*: this demands that we identify with Jesus self-sacrifice, but we can only identify with him because he first identified with us in our sin by taking our punishment.

- *The cross as victory*: we can share Jesus' victory only if we are united with him. We cannot be united with him unless our sins are forgiven. Our sins are forgiven because Jesus has taken our punishment for us, as our substitute.

The Cross as Moral Example

Another model of the atonement, first formulated by Augustine and restated by Peter Abelard at the beginning of the 12th century in reaction against Anselm's Satisfaction theory, is the Moral Example model. It is much favoured by modern liberal theologians.

This model proposes that Jesus died, not to appease or placate God, but to show human beings the depth of God's love for them. The purpose was to lead people to repentance. Thus, the atonement is not aimed at the appeasement of God's honour or justice, but at the moral improvement of humankind.

The theory has been criticised on the grounds that:

- It does not explain the crucifixion. Jesus did not need to die in order to provide people with a perfect moral example. He could have done so by his life and teachings.

- It teaches that human beings can achieve salvation through their own moral effort. It thus teaches salvation through works, not through faith, and denies the supernatural effect of the death of Jesus.

- It belittles God's anger against sin.

Key quote

Our redemption through the suffering of Christ … secures for us the true liberty of the children of God, in order that we might do all things out of love rather than out of fear – love for him that has shown us such grace. (Abelard)

quickfire

2.15 Name six theories of the atonement.

AO1 Activity

On small revision cards summarise the key features of each model of atonement. Support the explanations with extracts from quotes. This will help you select and recall a core set of points to develop in an answer to explaining each model and ensure that you are making 'accurate use of specialist language and vocabulary in context' (L5 band descriptor AO1).

Study tip

Make sure that you always answer the question set, paying particular attention to key words. This will ensure that you have the best chance of giving 'an extensive and relevant response which answers the specific demands of the question set' (L5 band descriptor AO1).

AO1 Developing skills

It is now time to reflect upon the information that has been covered so far. It is also important to consider how what you have learned can be focused and used for examination-style answers by practising the skills associated with AO1.

Assessment objective 1 (AO1) involves demonstrating knowledge and understanding. The terms 'knowledge' and 'understanding' are obvious but it is crucial to be familiar with how certain skills demonstrate these terms, and also, how the performance of these skills is measured (see generic band descriptors Band 5 for AS AO1).

▶ **Your new task is this:** below is a strong answer that has been written in response to a question requiring an examination of the objections made to the main models of atonement. Using the band level descriptors you can compare this with the relevant higher bands and the descriptions inside those bands. It is obviously a strong answer and so would not be in bands 1–3. In order to do this it will be useful to consider what is good about the answer and what is accurate. In analysing the answer's strengths, in a group, think of five things that make this answer a good one. You may have more than five observations and indeed suggestions to make it a perfect answer!

Answer

There are three main models of the atonement – Sacrifice, Penal Substitution and Moral Example. There are also variant models. The Sacrifice model has a variant Ransom model, which was further developed in 1931 by the Swedish theologian Gustaf Aulén into the *Christus Victor* model. The Penal Substitution model is a development of an earlier Satisfaction model.

Early theologians saw Jesus' death as a sacrifice for human sin. Basing their views on Old Testament ideas of sacrifice (the story of Abraham and Isaac in Genesis; the scapegoat in Leviticus) and on the Jewish Passover lamb, they argued that human beings had nothing they could sacrifice to God for their sins, but God had provided the 'pure victim' for them in Jesus.

Based on indications in the Gospels that Jesus himself thought of his death in terms of a ransom payment to redeem human beings from sin, Origen in the 2nd century developed the Sacrificial model into a Ransom model, maintaining that Jesus' death was a ransom payment to Satan. 'The payment,' he wrote, 'could not be made to God, because God was not holding sinners in captivity'.

Anselm, who was Archbishop of Canterbury in the 11th century, developed the Ransom model into the Satisfaction model, arguing that because people's debt to God was greater than they could pay, God had to pay the debt himself. And because the payment would not redeem human beings unless it was made by a human, God became a human being in Jesus so that he could pay the debt to himself and satisfy his offended honour.

The 16th-century Protestant reformers changed the basis of Anselm's Satisfaction model from the concept of God's honour to that of God's justice. Basing their argument mostly on the descriptions of vicarious suffering in the Suffering Servant Songs in the Old Testament Book of Isaiah, they proposed the alternative Penal Substitution model: that Jesus freed human beings from being punished for their sins by taking that punishment upon himself on the cross, thus satisfying the justice of God.

Key skills
Knowledge involves:

Selection of a range of (thorough) accurate and relevant information that is directly related to the specific demands of the question.

This means you choose the correct information relevant to the question set NOT the topic area. You will have to think and focus on selecting key information and NOT writing everything you know about the topic area.

Understanding involves:

Explanation that is extensive, demonstrating depth and/or breadth with excellent use of evidence and examples including (where appropriate) thorough and accurate supporting use of sacred texts, sources of wisdom and specialist language.

This means that you demonstrate that you understand something by being able to illustrate and expand your points through examples/supporting evidence in a personal way and NOT repeat chunks from a text book (known as rote learning).

Further application of skills:

Go through the topic areas in this section and create some bullet lists of key points from key areas. For each one, provide further elaboration and explanation through the use of evidence and examples.

Peter Abelard argued that the atonement was a Moral Example and this explanation is much favoured by modern liberal theologians

The Ransom model was further modified in 1931 by Aulén, who saw Jesus' death as 'a victory over the powers which hold mankind in bondage: sin, death, and the devil'. For him, the atonement is not the payment of a debt of honour to God or a vicarious punishment, but a victory by which Jesus triumphs over the powers of evil.

Finally, there is the Moral Example model, mostly associated with the 12th-century theologian Peter Abelard. This model proposes that Jesus died to show human beings the depth of God's love for them and lead them to repentance.

Many people have objected to the Sacrificial model on the grounds that no loving God would offer his only Son as a sacrifice in order to satisfy his own sense of justice.

The Ransom model has been criticised on the grounds that it makes Satan more powerful than he is and that it makes God both a debtor and a deceiver.

Anselm's Satisfaction model is considered flawed by some because it was based on an unbiblical, medieval concept of 'honour' which sees God as a feudal overlord.

The Penal Substitution model is also widely criticised as it is often seen as being based more on a criminal justice system than on the Bible. Moreover, no criminal justice system would justify punishing the innocent. It thus portrays God as an unreasonable, vengeful God. It has also been criticised for separating the Father and the Son – the Son steps in to save people from the Father. According to the theologian Jeffrey John, 'it made God sound like a psychopath'.

Aulén's *Christus Victor* model has been criticised on the grounds that it plays down human sin and is triumphalist.

Despite being favoured by liberal theologians, many find the Moral Example model flawed because it does not explain why Jesus had to die. It leans too much in the direction of salvation through works, and belittles God's anger against sin.

The Christian Church has no agreed doctrine of the atonement. Despite their shortcomings, all three main models, and their variants, are attempts by finite human minds to interpret the mind of God.

Issues for analysis and evaluation

The extent to which the three images of the atonement are contradictory

This section covers AO2 content and skills

Specification content

The extent to which the three images of the atonement are contradictory.

The three images propose totally different means of salvation and some have called this a contradictory and incoherent collection.

For instance, the Moral Example model teaches that salvation can be achieved through personal moral effort. Advocates of the Moral Example theory claim that the theory was taught in the 3rd century CE, whereas the Penal Substitution theory did not appear until the 16th century and so they argue that this is the original basis for any atonement model. Whilst they do not see any inconsistency, there is a sense of priority in understanding.

Advocates of the Moral Example theory maintain that their position is supported by New Testament teaching on the necessity of repentance for salvation and that this is the very foundation of Christian faith. Liberal Christians tend to favour the Moral Example theory.

However, the Sacrificial and Penal Substitution theories teach that salvation can be achieved only through the death of Christ and our faith in him. Advocates of the Sacrificial and Penal Substitution theories maintain that their position is supported by New Testament teaching on the necessity of faith for salvation and, although the Penal Substitution theory was not systematically proposed until the 16th century, its origins are found in the New Testament itself. Indeed, the Sacrificial model is much earlier and has its origins in the Old Testament. Conservative Christians tend to favour the Sacrificial or Penal Substitution theories.

However, in *The Cross of Christ* (1986), the evangelical theologian John R.W. Stott proposed that the Moral Example model can be seen as part of the Penal Substitution model. Whereas the Penal Substitution theory focuses entirely on the death of Jesus, the Moral Example theory sees Jesus' death in the wider context of his ethical teaching. Jesus was sentenced to die because of what he taught. Thus, Moral Example and Penal Substitution are interconnected within the larger story of Jesus' incarnation, crucifixion and resurrection.

It is claimed that the Moral Example model clashes with Paul's rejection of salvation through works. Some would see this understanding as dangerous and firmly rejected in New Testament writings.

This, however, may be resolved if we accept that Paul was referring to Jewish ritual 'works' (e.g. circumcision, dietary rules) and not to good works in general. Salvation through works (personal morality, faithfulness to Jesus' teaching) can thus be harmonised with salvation through faith in what Jesus achieved through his sacrificial death.

In addition, the New Testament itself suggests that, in the words of James, 'you foolish person, do you want evidence that faith without deeds is useless?' and 'show me your faith without deeds, and I will show you my faith by my deeds', which suggests that the tension between salvation by faith and salvation through personal moral effort are not separate theories.

The three images are not contradictory, nor are they mutually exclusive. They all help to bring out different aspects of the atonement.

One possible conclusion could be that, although there may be debate about which is the most important understanding of the atonement, each understanding serves to support the other rather than contradict it outright. It could be considered unfair to accept a conclusion that they are contradictory in the light of this, unless of course, one takes a very narrow and dogmatic stance that to embrace another understanding would impair theological thinking and cause confusion, uncertainty and heresy. It is perhaps doubtful that the latter view could ever be justified or supported by many.

AO2 Activity *Possible lines of argument*

Listed below are some conclusions that could be drawn from the AO2 reasoning in the above text:

1. The three images of the atonement (Sacrifice/Ransom; Satisfaction/Penal Substitution; Moral Example) are contradictory.

2. The three images of the atonement can be harmonised.

3. It does not matter whether the three images are contradictory or not. They reflect the mystery of the atonement

Consider each of the conclusions drawn above and collect evidence and examples to support each argument from the AO1 and AO2 material studied in this section. Select one conclusion that you think is most convincing and explain why it is so. Now contrast this with the weakest conclusion in the list, justifying your argument with clear reasoning and evidence.

Specification content

The extent to which the three images suggest that the Christian God is cruel.

The extent to which the three images suggest that the Christian God is cruel

Some have argued that all three images of atonement could be interpreted as suggesting that the Christian God is a cruel God.

For instance, the Sacrificial model portrays Jesus' death in terms of the Old Testament scapegoat or Passover lamb. It follows that a God who offers his own Son as a sacrifice in order to satisfy his own sense of justice is an angry tyrant who must be appeased before he forgives. The variant Ransom model makes God both a deceiver and a debtor.

As regards the Satisfaction model, based on medieval concepts, it depicts God as a feudal overlord who is more concerned with his own hurt pride than with the hurt experienced by his Son. The reformers' Penal Substitution theory simply replaced Anselm's concept of God's offended honour with the concept of God's offended justice. It portrays God as a vengeful God who perpetrates 'a form of cosmic child abuse' against his Son. God appears, therefore, to be a God of retribution, inconsistent with presentations as a God of love, mercy and forgiveness.

In addition, neither does the Moral Example model explain the passion and crucifixion. For example, if all Jesus did was to provide people with a perfect moral example, why did he have to die? What does this tell us about God?

These are all serious accusations against am omnibenevolent God.

However, others would argue that none of the three models necessarily show a cruel God. In defence of this view it could be argued that the very word 'atonement' expresses the idea that there was a need for sinful humanity to be reconciled with God. In line with this reasoning, Jesus' death was God's way of achieving this reconciliation. It was part of his eternal plan to save humanity. Moreover, it was not the end, because three days later Jesus was resurrected. This clearly shows God's love for both humanity and his Son. In a sense, despite apparent inconsistencies raised in analysis parts of the story, the full and complete picture and understanding emerge at the end – the end justifies the means.

In addition, the Sacrificial/and Ransom models emphasise that Jesus willingly died for his enemies. Augustine writes, 'where did he find that offering, the pure victim that he would offer? He offered himself'. In this context, we need to remember that as Jesus himself is God, the sacrifice for humanity causes suffering to God himself. The Satisfaction/Penal Substitution model emphasises that Jesus died the death that sinners deserved. This must be the ultimate example of divine love.

The Moral Example model in particular emphasises that Jesus accepted an undeserved death. This was a demonstration of love that moves Christians to repent and thus reconciles them with God.

In conclusion, one possible solution could be that despite serious accusations of cruelty charged against the Christian God, these can only be upheld when focusing on parts of the picture. The best defence of the Christian God, it would appear according to this line of reasoning, is to see the picture in its entirety and the end result.

AO2 Activity *Possible lines of argument*

Listed below are some conclusions that could be drawn from the AO2 reasoning in the accompanying text:

1. All three models of the atonement portray the Christian God as a cruel God.

2. Only some of the models of the atonement portray the Christian God as a cruel God.

3. Not one of the three models of the atonement portrays the Christian God as a cruel God. In fact, they all demonstrate his love both for humanity and for his Son.

Consider each of the conclusions drawn above and collect evidence and examples to support each argument from the AO1 and AO2 material studied in this section. Select one conclusion that you think is most convincing and explain why it is so. Now contrast this with the weakest conclusion in the list, justifying your argument with clear reasoning and evidence.

AO2 Developing skills

It is now time to reflect upon the information that has been covered so far. It is also important to consider how what you have learned can be focused and used for examination-style answers by practising the skills associated with AO2.

Assessment objective 2 (AO2) involves 'analysis' and 'evaluation'. The terms may be obvious but it is crucial to be familiar with how certain skills demonstrate these terms, and also, how the performance of these skills is measured (see generic band descriptors Band 5 for AS AO2).

Obviously an answer is placed within an appropriate band descriptor depending upon how well the answer performs, ranging from excellent, good, satisfactory, basic/limited to very limited.

▶ **Your task is this:** below is a reasonable answer, although not perfect, that has been written in response to a question requiring an examination of whether or not the Moral Example theory is a convincing model of the atonement. Using the band level descriptors you can compare this with the relevant higher bands and the descriptions inside those bands. It is obviously a reasonable answer and so would not be in bands 5, 1 or 2. In order to do this it will be useful to consider what is both strong and weak about the answer and therefore what needs developing.

In analysing the answer, in a group, identify three ways to make this answer a better one. You may have more than three observations and indeed suggestions to make it a perfect answer!

Answer

At first glance, the Moral Example theory is a very convincing model of the atonement.

First, it removes the risk of portraying God in a negative light, as most other theories do. For example, the early theories that Jesus died as a sacrifice for human sin (Hebrews), or that his death was a ransom payment to Satan (Origen), present God either as a tyrant or as a debtor and deceiver, and the 16th-century reformers' Penal Substitution portrays him as an unjust child abuser.

Second, it gives human beings responsibility for following Jesus' moral example. With other models, human beings have no part in the process of salvation. All the work is done by Jesus.

Third, it does not allege that Jesus' death had any 'supernatural' effect. This makes the atonement more acceptable to those who call for the demythologisation of the supernatural aspects of the Gospel message.

On further examination, however, the Moral Example theory is not so convincing.

First, it does not explain why Jesus had to die. He could have given his followers the necessary moral example in his life and teaching.

Second, it teaches salvation through works, not faith. Human beings can now secure their own salvation simply through their own moral effort by following Jesus' example. This goes against the idea of justification through faith, one of the cardinal beliefs of the Protestant Reformation.

Third, it diminishes God's anger against sin. If Jesus' death was not in some way a vicarious death for the punishment of human sin, then the Fall has not been erased and God's justice has still not been administered and satisfied.

Key skills

Analysis involves identifying issues raised by the materials in the AO1, together with those identified in the AO2 section, and presents sustained and clear views, either of scholars or from a personal perspective ready for evaluation.

This means that it picks out key things to debate and the lines of argument presented by others or a personal point of view.

Evaluation involves considering the various implications of the issues raised based upon the evidence gleaned from analysis and provides an extensive detailed argument with a clear conclusion.

This means that the answer weighs up the various and different lines of argument analysed through individual commentary and response and arrives at a conclusion through a clear process of reasoning.

T3 Religious life

Specification content

Luther's arguments for justification by faith alone (with reference to Romans 1:17; 5:1; Ephesians 2:8–9; Galatians 2:16; and Luther's rejection of James 2:24).

quickfire

3.1 What does the word *justification* mean?

Key terms

Absolution: declaration by a priest that a person's sins have been forgiven

Salvation: deliverance from God's judgement of sin

Key person

Martin Luther (1483–1546): the founder of the Protestant Reformation in Europe.

A: Faith and works

Make sure you have read and understood the set texts: Romans 1:17, 5:1; Galatians 2:16; Ephesians 2:8–9; James 2:24.

Luther and justification by faith alone

One of the greatest problems for Christian believers is that of justification. 'Justification' means being made righteous in the sight of God.

In the Middle Ages, the Roman Catholic Church linked justification with baptism and penance. In baptism, God began the process of making an individual righteous in his sight by removing original sin. The process was continued by confession and penance. People confessed their sins to a priest, who granted them absolution for any actual sins that they had committed and imposed a penance that they must perform. The idea was thus formed that penance led to righteousness, that justification was an appropriate reward for good works.

Closely associated with the doctrine of penance was that of purgatory. The Roman Catholic Church taught that if Christians died without having done adequate penance for their sins, they had to spend time in purgatory to complete that penance. Only then would they be accepted into heaven. Purgatory, therefore, was a place of suffering where the souls of believers expiated their sins.

Martin Luther was a German Augustinian monk and professor of theology at the University of Wittenberg who felt a deep sense of sinfulness and a profound anxiety for his soul's salvation. Despite doing everything that the church required of him and spending long hours in prayer, confession and penance, he felt he was losing touch with God, and fell into a deep spiritual despair.

Martin Luther

Eventually, he came to the conclusion that, far from being a process in which human beings had a part, justification was entirely the gift of God. Sinners are not saved by good works. They are saved by faith alone (Luther's term for this was *sola fide*), by absolute dependence on God's promise of forgiveness. God then makes them righteous. Luther based this conviction on Paul's words in his Epistle to the Romans (1:17): 'The one who is righteous will live by faith'. There was further support in Romans 5:1 ('we are justified by faith'); Galatians 2:16 ('we know that a person is justified not by the works of law but through faith in Jesus Christ') and Ephesians 2:8–9; ('by grace you have been saved through faith, and this is not your own doing; it is the gift of God – not the result of works, so that no one may boast').

It was true, however, that other biblical passages contradicted these Pauline statements. The Epistle of James (2:24), for instance, maintains that 'a person is justified by works and not faith alone'. Luther failed to reconcile this with the Pauline assertions, but concluded that the Epistle of James was 'an Epistle of straw' that had 'nothing of the nature of the Gospel about it'. For Luther, faith was a vital, transforming power, a new and invigorating personal relationship with God.

In 1517 Luther was able to apply his new theory of salvation to a church practice that was an obvious abuse. This was the sale of indulgences. An indulgence was a piece of paper issued by the Pope which granted a sinner remission from penance for a payment. The proceeds from the sale of indulgences went towards the building of the church of St Peter in Rome, although in Wittenberg half the money went to the Cardinal Archbishop of Mainz to offset what he had paid for his appointment to the archbishopric.

A commissioner for this collection was Johann Tetzel, a Dominican monk. Tetzel overstated Catholic doctrine on indulgences, alleging that they not only liberated the living from doing penance, but also that the souls of the dead could be released from purgatory on payment of a few coins by their surviving relatives. A well known jingle was attributed to him: 'As soon as a coin in the coffer rings / the soul from purgatory springs'.

Study tip

Good candidates understand that the selling of indulgences to shorten the time spent by sinners in purgatory was a distortion of Catholic teaching, preached by a rogue individual, Johann Tetzel.

To Luther, convinced that salvation was a matter of a right personal relationship with God, Tetzel's teaching was an abomination. He preached against the abuse of indulgences, and on 31 October 1517 posted on the door of the castle church in Wittenberg his famous Ninety-five Theses against clerical abuses in the Roman Catholic Church. This was the spark that ignited the Protestant Reformation.

AO1 Activity

Draw a clear diagram to illustrate how Martin Luther's understanding of justification differed from that of the Roman Catholic Church. Show how each of the elements are related. This will mean that you have an understanding of the different aspects of doctrines of justification and an awareness of the key terminology involved. This demonstrates 'accurate use of specialist language' (AO1 Level 5 band descriptor).

quickfire

3.2 What is the Latin term for *by faith alone*?

Key quote

We do not become righteous by doing righteous deeds but, having been made righteous, we do righteous deeds. (Luther)

quickfire

3.3 What was an *indulgence*?

Key quote

What then shall we say? That the Gentiles, who did not pursue righteousness, have obtained it, a righteousness that is by faith; but the people of Israel, who pursued the law as the way of righteousness, have not attained their goal. Why not? Because they pursued it not by faith but as if it were by works. They stumbled over the stumbling stone. (Romans 9:30–32)

The Council of Trent as a response to Luther

From 1545 to 1563 the Roman Catholic Church held an important council, known as the Council of Trent (Trent or Trento is a city in what is now northern Italy), to consider its response to the Reformation. On the subject of justification, the Council considered the following questions:

- Is justification the gift of God or does it require human effort?
- What is the relationship between faith and good works?
- What is the relation between justification and the sacraments?
- Can people know that they are justified?
- Can people earn justification through works?

In 1547 it concluded that:

- God does not just make people righteous; they must become righteous.
- Good works are required as a condition for ultimate justification.
- People cannot bring about their own salvation; they must cooperate with the grace of God.

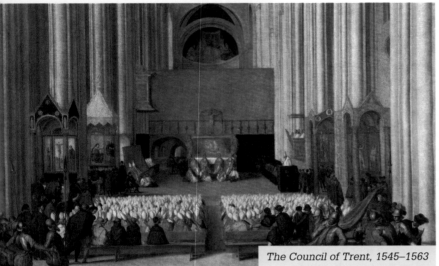

The Council of Trent, 1545–1563

- Justification works in two phases. In the first phase, righteousness is mediated through baptism, which is God's gift of grace. In the second, righteousness is increased by participation in the Eucharist and penance, and by doing good works.
- There is a middle position between assurance of salvation and despair. People can have a relative (not absolute) certainty of justification.
- Neither faith nor works can be said to merit justification. Initial justification is by grace, but works are necessary for progressive salvation.

Protestant criticism of the Council of Trent

There are biblical grounds to support the doctrine that God acquits sinners of guilt in the sense of not counting their sins against them. There is an example in II Corinthians 5:19, where Paul says: 'in Christ God was reconciling the world to himself, not counting their trespasses against them'. Justification is thus a declarative act of God's grace.

Trent proclaimed that 'by his good works the justified man acquires a claim to supernatural reward from God'. This contradicts biblical teaching that good works do not merit grace. Grace is a gift. It is unmerited. People work not for a gift but for wages.

Trent declared that to 'those who work well unto the end, … life eternal is … a recompense … to their good works and merit'. This contradicts biblical teaching that eternal life is 'the gift of God' (Romans 6:23) and is available right now to those who believe (John 5:24). John 6:29 states clearly that the only 'work' necessary for salvation is to believe.

Christian believers work not in order to receive salvation but because they have already received it. Good works are not necessary for salvation, but salvation inevitably produces good works.

quickfire

3.4 What, according to the Council of Trent, are the two phases of justification?

Key quote

If any one says … that no one is truly justified but he who believes himself justified; and that, by this faith alone, absolution and justification are effected; let him be anathema.

(Council of Trent, Canon XIV)

AO1 Activity

Create a table with three columns. In Column 1 insert the questions on justification that the Council of Trent attempted to answer. In Column 2, insert Trent's response. In Column 3, insert Protestant criticisms of Trent's response.

A modern view: E.P. Sanders

In his *Paul and Palestinian Judaism* (1977), E.P. Sanders argues that the Jewish religion, in which Paul had been brought up, was not simply a salvation by works religion. On the contrary, there was in Judaism 'a pattern of religion', which Sanders calls covenantal nomism. This was the Jews' belief that God had instigated a covenant of grace with them, which made them a 'chosen nation' and gave them a special status. They maintained their status in that covenant, however, only by obeying God's commandments. The purpose of keeping God's law was therefore to maintain the status. The status itself was a gift, not a reward for obedience. So Jews entered the covenant by grace and stayed in by works. This, Sanders argues, was the normative Jewish view in Paul's time.

Sanders sets Paul's theology in this light. He maintains that Paul worked his way from solution to problem. The solution is that in Jesus God has acted to save the world. The problem therefore must be that the world is in need of salvation. But God also gave the Mosaic law. If Jesus is given for salvation, it must follow that the Mosaic law was not.

The problem with the Mosaic law was not that it failed to make those who kept it righteous, but that it gave them the wrong kind of righteousness. It excluded Gentiles and led the Jews to boast in their ethnicity and election as the people of God.

Paul realised that people are justified not through the Mosaic law but through the cross of Jesus. The justification that Jesus achieved for men and women was an act of God's grace. It was not earned by humankind. It can only be maintained, however, when men and women respond in gratitude, keeping God's commandments and entering into a mystical participation in Jesus. In Sanders' words, 'Christ came to provide a new Lordship for those who participate in his death and resurrection', be they Jews or Gentiles. Thus, Christians enter the new covenant by baptism, but must thereafter be made righteous by faith.

Some theologians have criticised Sanders' theory on the grounds that:

- It uses non-biblical, rabbinic sources to over-ride biblical teaching.

- It explains away contradictory evidence; e.g. the rabbinic literature of Paul's time contains ample evidence of a Jewish belief in righteousness by works.

- It fails to address the problem of self-righteousness – people who believe themselves morally superior to their peers because they adhere strictly to God's commandments.

AO1 Activity

Draw a diagram to illustrate the similarities and differences between E.P. Sanders' view of justification and that of: (a) the Roman Catholic Church and (b) Luther.

Study tip

Always make sure that you know what the Bible teaches in support of the different doctrines on justification. The band descriptor for AO1 (Level 5) expects 'Thorough and accurate reference made to sacred texts and sources of wisdom, where appropriate'.

Specification content

E. P. Sanders and the role of works in justification.

Key terms

Covenantal nomism: God's election of the Jews as a chosen nation provided they obeyed his commandments

Rabbinic: relating to the teachings of Jewish rabbis

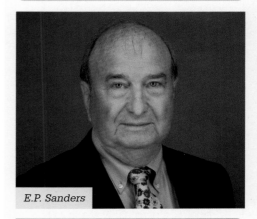

E.P. Sanders

Key person

E.P. Sanders (born 1937): is an American New Testament scholar who has contributed much to a new understanding of the writings of Paul.

quickfire

3.5 What did E.P. Sanders call the pattern of religion which he found in Judaism?

Key quote

Briefly put, covenantal nomism is the view that one's place in God's plan is established on the basis of the covenant and that the covenant requires as the proper response of man his obedience to its commandments, while providing means of atonement for transgression. (E.P. Sanders)

Key skills

Knowledge involves:

Selection of a range of (thorough) accurate and relevant information that is directly related to the specific demands of the question.

This means you choose the correct information relevant to the question set NOT the topic area. You will have to think and focus on selecting key information and NOT writing everything you know about the topic area.

Understanding involves:

Explanation that is extensive, demonstrating depth and/or breadth with excellent use of evidence and examples including (where appropriate) thorough and accurate supporting use of sacred texts, sources of wisdom and specialist language.

This means that you demonstrate that you understand something by being able to illustrate and expand your points through examples/supporting evidence in a personal way and NOT repeat chunks from a text book (known as rote learning).

Further application of skills:

Go through the topic areas in this section and create some bullet lists of key points from key areas. For each one, provide further elaboration and explanation through the use of evidence and examples.

AO1 Developing skills

It is now time to reflect upon the information that has been covered so far. It is also important to consider how what you have learned can be focused and used for examination-style answers by practising the skills associated with AO1.

Assessment objective 1 (AO1) involves demonstrating knowledge and understanding. The terms 'knowledge' and 'understanding' are obvious but it is crucial to be familiar with how certain skills demonstrate these terms, and also, how the performance of these skills is measured (see generic band descriptors Band 5 for AS AO1).

▶ **Your new task is this:** below is a below average answer that has been written in response to a question requiring an examination of how Luther's doctrine of justification differed from that of the Roman Catholic Church. It is obviously a below average answer and so would be about band 2. It will be useful, initially, to consider what is missing from the answer and what is inaccurate. The accompanying list gives you some possible observations to assist you. Be aware, as not all points may be relevant! In analysing the answer's weaknesses, in a group, choose five points from the list that you would use to improve the answer in order to make it stronger. Then write out your additions, each one in a clear paragraph, remembering the principles of explaining with evidence and/ or examples. You may add more of your own suggestions, but try to negotiate as a group and prioritise the most important things to add.

Answer

The Roman Catholic Church linked justification with baptism. In baptism, God made people righteous by removing original sin. If people did actually sin, they could confess their sin to a priest, who imposed a penance. If they died without having completed their penance, they had to spend time in purgatory.

Martin Luther came to the conclusion that human beings had no part in justification. Sinners are not saved by good works. They are saved by faith alone. He found support for this teaching in the Letters of Paul.

The Roman Catholic Council of Trent met to consider the church's response to Luther. It concluded that good works are needed for justification. People must become righteous through their own efforts.

Protestants criticised Trent's findings on the grounds that there is biblical support for justification by faith.

Observations

1. An introduction is needed setting out what 'justification' means.
2. There is no explanation that baptism is merely the first stage of the process.
3. There is no mention of absolution.
4. The link between penance and good works is ignored.
5. A brief introduction is needed into who Martin Luther was.
6. There is no explanation of how Luther came to this conclusion or what specific support for his ideas he found in the Pauline Letters.
7. There is no explanation of the Council of Trent's insistence that justification is a two-stage process – first baptism, then partaking of the sacraments.
8. No examples are given of the alleged biblical support for the doctrine of justification by faith.

Issues for analysis and evaluation

The extent to which the New Testament letters support arguments for justification by faith alone

This section covers AO2 content and skills

Specification content

The extent to which the New Testament letters support arguments for justification by faith alone.

Theologians who argue against the doctrine of justification by faith alone insist that it is unbiblical. There are many New Testament verses, not only in the Letters but in the Gospels and the Book of Acts as well, that appear to reject it. In the Sermon on the Mount, for example, Jesus says: 'let your light shine before others, so that they may see your good works', and in his sermon in Acts 26, Paul says that people 'should repent … turn to God and do deeds consistent with repentance'.

In the Letters specifically, Paul instructs the Romans that it will be 'the doers of the law [who]… will be justified'. The Epistle to the Hebrews says that 'by faith Abraham obeyed'. So his justification was due not to faith alone, but also to obedience. The Epistle of James confirms that Abraham's works were essential to his justification.

Significantly, the phrase 'by faith alone' occurs only in James 2:24, where it is used to assert that 'a person is justified by works and not by faith alone'. Luther stands accused of having added the word 'alone' to Paul's statement in Romans 1:17 that the 'The one who is righteous will live by faith'.

The New Testament sees justification as a process; the doctrine of *sola fide* sees it as a one-off past event. It is an antinomian doctrine. Antinomianism teaches that Christians are not obliged to keep any of the Mosaic laws, whereas the Council of Jerusalem agreed that Christians are obliged to keep all of the Mosaic laws except those that have to do with Jewish ritual, regulations and ceremonies.

Theologians who support the doctrine of justification by faith would answer that there are many New Testament verses that endorse it, not only in the Letters but in the Gospels and the Book of Acts as well. When, for example, Jesus is asked in the Gospel of John what people must do to perform the works of God?, he answers, 'This is the work of God, that you believe in him whom he has sent'. This suggests that all one has to do to acquire salvation is to believe. When Paul and Silas are asked by their jailer in Acts 16 what one must do to be saved, they answer, 'Believe in the Lord Jesus, and you will be saved'. They do not mention works.

In the Letters, particularly the Pauline Letters, there are several verses that support the doctrine. For example, in Romans 1:17, and again in Galatians 3:11, Paul quotes the prophet Habakuk: 'The one who is righteous will live by faith'. In Romans 4, he argues that Abraham was the Old Covenant's model of salvation by faith alone. In the New Covenant, God declares sinners righteous by imputing to them the righteousness of Jesus.

In Romans 5, Paul asserts that since 'we are justified by faith, we have peace with God through our Lord Jesus Christ', and in Philippians 3, he writes of 'not having a righteousness of my own which comes from the law, but one that comes through faith in Christ, the righteousness from God based on faith'.

Support for the doctrine is scarce in other Letters, although the Epistle to the Hebrews makes the same quotation from Habakuk as that quoted by Paul in Romans and Galatians.

However, supporters of the doctrine insist that it focuses on what God has achieved through Jesus, and not on what humans can achieve for themselves. This is why Luther considered it to be 'the article by which the church stands'.

AO2 Activity *Possible lines of argument*

Listed below are some conclusions that could be drawn from the AO2 reasoning in the above text:

1. Justification by faith alone is rejected in the New Testament Letters.
2. Justification by faith alone is endorsed by the New Testament letters.
3. Justification by faith alone is neither rejected nor endorsed in the New Testament letters.

Consider each of the conclusions drawn above and collect evidence and examples to support each argument from the AO1 and AO2 material studied in this section. Select one conclusion that you think is most convincing and explain why it is so. Now contrast this with the weakest conclusion in the list, justifying your argument with clear reasoning and evidence.

Specification content

The extent to which both faith and works are aspects of justification.

The extent to which both faith and works are aspects of justification

Some people would argue that both faith and works are aspects of justification. Justification, they say, is a gradual, cooperative process between God and sinners. It is sacerdotal, i.e. it is accomplished through the sacraments of the church.

They accept that the process begins with God's free gift of baptism, which removes original sin, but it must then be constantly maintained by repentance, penance, prayer, and good works. If this is not the case, there is no point for a Christian to try to keep God's Law.

James (2:24) clarifies the issue when he says that justification 'is by works and not faith alone'. James' argument puts people in control of their destiny and appeals to their inherent sense of justice. People can only be declared righteous when they are righteous.

If God declares people to be righteous when they are not righteous, God is guilty of deceit and compromises his own justice. This is 'legal fiction'.

Others believe that justification is a one-off, past event. It is forensic, i.e. it is an act of God that makes sinners holy.

Nothing that sinners ever do can justify them before God. They can never satisfy God's Law. They can therefore be justified only through a divine act – God declaring them righteous. This God has done once for all through Jesus. Justification is based entirely on the sacrifice of Jesus. It is a gift of God's grace and is received through faith.

James' argument in 2.24 is that 'dead faith' is worthless. Dead faith is merely an intellectual acceptance of Jesus. It causes no change in a person's life. Real faith produces good works. But good works are the result of justification, not its cause.

If justification depended on human effort, people would be constantly engaged in a futile struggle to be good enough in the sight of God. This would lead to bondage to God's Law and to the potential for boasting if people thought they were doing well.

There is no 'legal fiction'. God's justice has not been compromised because in the atonement, God has counted people's sins against Jesus. If this were not so, all individuals would have to atone for their own sins.

The compromise for some Christians is to see that by repentance, penance, prayer and good works are all the flip side of the faith coin. In other words, as James writes, it is impossible for faith not to have any impact upon one's life. This is not to say that it is by good works that Christians are saved, but simply that, as James writes, 'the evidence' of faith is good works. This position still maintains justification by faith alone and is in line with Paul's teachings.

In conclusion, one possible solution could be that it is a matter of emphasis and interpretation in combining faith and works, but it is interesting to see that neither side of the debate would suggest that it is by good works alone that a Christian is saved. Faith, therefore, seems to have the upper hand in determining justification.

AO2 Activity Possible lines of argument

Listed below are some conclusions that could be drawn from the AO2 reasoning in the above text:

1. Justification can be earned through human effort.

2. Justification can only be imputed by God.

3. Justification depends on both faith and works.

Consider each of the conclusions drawn above and collect evidence and examples to support each argument from the AO1 and AO2 material studied in this section. Select one conclusion that you think is most convincing and explain why it is so. Now contrast this with the weakest conclusion in the list, justifying your argument with clear reasoning and evidence.

AO2 Developing skills

It is now time to reflect upon the information that has been covered so far. It is also important to consider how what you have learned can be focused and used for examination-style answers by practising the skills associated with AO2.

Assessment objective 2 (AO2) involves 'analysis' and 'evaluation'. The terms may be obvious but it is crucial to be familiar with how certain skills demonstrate these terms, and also, how the performance of these skills is measured (see generic band descriptors Band 5 for AS AO2).

Obviously an answer is placed within an appropriate band descriptor depending upon how well the answer performs, ranging from excellent, good, satisfactory, basic/limited to very limited.

▶ **Your new task is this:** below is a below average answer that has been written in response to a question requiring an evaluation of whether E.P. Sanders' view of justification is convincing. It is obviously a below average answer and so would be about lower band 2. It will be useful, initially, to consider what is missing from the answer and what is inaccurate. The accompanying list gives you some possible observations to assist you. Be aware, as not all points may be relevant! In analysing the answer's weaknesses, in a group, choose five points from the list that you would use to improve the answer in order to make it stronger. Then write out your additions, each one in a clear paragraph. Remember, it is how you use the points that is the most important factor. Apply the principles of evaluation by making sure that you: identify issues clearly; present accurate views of others making sure that you comment on the views presented; reach an overall personal judgement. You may add more of your own suggestions, but try to negotiate as a group and prioritise the most important things to add.

Answer

E.P. Sanders argues that in the Jewish religion, in which St Paul was brought up, there was a 'pattern' based on the Jews' belief that God had instigated a covenant with them, which made them a 'chosen nation'. They maintained this covenant by obeying God's commandments. Thus, the covenant itself was a gift, but it was maintained by obedience.

Sanders sets Paul's theology in this light. Paul realised that people are justified not through the Mosaic law but through the cross. The justification that Jesus achieved for humanity was an act of God's grace and can only be maintained when people respond in obedience. Thus, Christians enter the new covenant by baptism, but must thereafter be made righteous by faith.

Some theologians have criticised Sanders' theory on the grounds that it uses non-biblical sources to over-ride biblical teaching. However, his position is valid because it reflects traditional thinking.

Observations

1. What is the title of Sanders' book on the subject?
2. What is Sanders' technical term for this 'pattern?
3. Where exactly does Paul say these things?
4. What are the non-biblical sources used by Sanders?
5. Are there other arguments against Sanders' views, e.g. evidence of a Jewish belief in justification by works? that it fails to address the problem of self-righteousness?
6. The one-sentence conclusion is superficial and invalid. The conclusion should be balanced, reflecting the argument presented and clearly linking to the question.

Key skills

Analysis involves identifying issues raised by the materials in the AO1, together with those identified in the AO2 section, and presents sustained and clear views, either of scholars or from a personal perspective ready for evaluation.

This means that it picks out key things to debate and the lines of argument presented by others or a personal point of view.

Evaluation involves considering the various implications of the issues raised based upon the evidence gleaned from analysis and provides an extensive detailed argument with a clear conclusion.

This means that the answer weighs up the various and different lines of argument analysed through individual commentary and response and arrives at a conclusion through a clear process of reasoning.

Specification content

The New Testament community of believers.

Key quote

They devoted themselves to the apostles' teaching and fellowship, to the breaking of bread and the prayers. (Acts 2:42)

Key terms

Didache: a Greek word meaning 'teaching'; what the apostles taught

Kerygma: a Greek word meaning 'proclamation'; what the apostles preached

Key quote

… the *kerygma* consists of the announcement of certain historical events in a setting which displays the significance of those events. The events in question are those of the appearance of Jesus in history – His ministry, sufferings and death and His subsequent manifestation of Himself to His followers as risen from the dead …– and the emergence of the Church as a society distinguished by the power and activity of the Holy Spirit …. (C.H. Dodd)

quickfire

3.6 What does the word *kerygma* mean?

B: The community of believers

Make sure you have read and understood the set text: Acts 2:42–47.

The New Testament community of believers

The Acts of the Apostles is the earliest account we have of the spread of Christianity during the 1st century CE. There is a general consensus that Acts was written by Luke, the author of the third Gospel, probably before 70 CE, no more than some forty years after the crucifixion of Jesus.

The life of the early Christian community is characterised mainly by its enthusiasm under the guidance of the Holy Spirit. From the beginning, however, it demonstrates elements of an organised structure, reflected in its practices, communal life, worship and discipline. These are described in Acts 2:42–47. We are told that the early Christians 'devoted themselves to the apostles' teaching and fellowship, to the breaking of bread and the prayers', and that 'they had all things in common'.

'They devoted themselves to the apostles' teaching and fellowship'

'The apostles' teaching' (Greek, *didache*) was preached in the early church in what the New Testament scholar C. H. Dodd and others have termed the *kerygma*, which means 'a proclamation'. The aim of the *kerygma* was to proclaim the key facts of the Gospel. It followed a particular pattern:

- Old Testament prophecies have been fulfilled; the Messiah has come.
- This has happened through the life, death and resurrection of Jesus.
- He was born of the house of David, and died to save humankind.
- He was buried, but resurrected on the third day, according to the Scriptures.
- He ascended to Heaven and sits on the right hand of God.
- He will come again to be humankind's Judge and Saviour.
- Therefore, all are called to repent and be baptised in his name.

This was the teaching to which the early Christian community was 'devoted'. It was united in its belief that Jesus was the Messiah, that he had been raised from the dead, that he now sits at the right hand of God and that it is through him that people's sins are forgiven. Acceptance of this teaching, and of baptism, led the believers to a 'fellowship', a special relationship with God through Jesus Christ, and with each other, expressed in partaking of communion, holding fast to the apostolic doctrines and following a particular way of life.

'[They devoted themselves] to the breaking of bread'

The phrase 'breaking of bread' can signify two things:

- The breaking of the bread at the Lord's Supper, the sacrament that Jesus himself had established as his memorial rite.
- The dividing of the loaves at a communal meal. In apostolic times, such meals were held regularly in some Jewish communities (e.g. the Essene community).

The meaning of the phrase is determined by its context.

- In Acts 2:42, which is used in the context of worship, it probably refers to the memorial of Jesus' death.
- In Acts 2:46 it probably refers to an early church practice that may well have been a means of providing sustenance for the poorer members of the church.

Both practices demonstrated the unity of the early Christian community; the first because it was a sacrament reflecting the members' communion with each other and with God; and the second because it allowed them to deepen their relationship with each other through charitable acts.

'[They devoted themselves] to the prayers'

Jewish men in Jerusalem went to the Temple to pray at least three times a day. The apostles and their followers still adhered to this custom. Acts 3:11 and Acts 5:12 record that they met 'in Solomon's portico', which was a roofed colonnade forming part of the Court of the Gentiles, so called because Gentiles were allowed to enter it.

However, the early Christians met also to pray in private homes. There may have been several reasons for this:

- The Pentecost experience had been so intense that it compelled them to seek constant fellowship with God and with each other.
- The practice brought them into contact with pious Jews who would then be introduced to Jesus as Messiah.
- They were aware that prayer was the main source of their strength as a community.

The word 'prayers' includes praise, adoration, thanksgiving, petition, confession and giving God glory.

'They had all things in common'

Acts 2:45 states that all those who believed 'would sell their possessions and goods and distribute the proceeds to all, as any had need'.

This, however, does not mean that the early Christian community taught some kind of religious communism, where 'all things in common' meant a redistribution of wealth. Nowhere in Acts is there any suggestion of class warfare or confiscation of property. The communal life is not compulsory for all Christians, because we read elsewhere in Acts that some believers owned property (e.g. in 12:12, the disciples meet in a house that belonged to Mary, Mark's mother).

What Luke is testifying to is the voluntary, loving, and selfless disposition of the early Christians. The Holy Spirit acting in their lives caused them to care for their less fortunate colleagues. Not everyone received a distribution of what was laid at the apostles' feet. The proceeds were distributed 'as any had need'. There was no general redistribution of wealth.

Nowhere else in the New Testament is there mention of a similar community to the one at Jerusalem. The experiment seems to have been restricted to the earliest years of Christianity and may have been a failure.

Key quote

They devoted themselves to the apostles' teaching and to fellowship, to the breaking of bread and to prayer. Everyone was filled with awe at the many wonders and signs performed by the apostles. All the believers were together and had everything in common. They sold property and possessions to give to anyone who had need. Every day they continued to meet together in the temple courts. They broke bread in their homes and ate together with glad and sincere hearts, praising God and enjoying the favour of all the people. And the Lord added to their number daily those who were being saved. (Acts 2:42–47)

Key term

The Pentecost experience: the pouring of the Holy Spirit on the apostles on the first Christian Pentecost, as described in Acts 2:1–13

Study tip

Remember to explain each point that you make in an examination answer to the full. Think carefully about each sentence and how it relates to the question and the previous sentence. Aim for at least three clear sentences to explain a concept or idea, giving examples from different sources to support your point. For development of the point, bring in a variety of ways in which the application of this principle is demonstrated and, if possible, introduce some contrasting scholarly views.

quickfire

3.7 What is known as 'the body of Christ' on earth?

quickfire

3.8 What does the word *sacrament* mean?

quickfire

3.9 What two sacraments are recognised by Protestants?

quickfire

3.10 In what two ways does the Christian church show God's grace?

The New Testament community of believers as a model for the contemporary church

The contemporary Christian church is 'the body of Christ' on earth. It exists to worship God, to administer the sacraments (rites that confer grace) and to evangelise the world. It is a sign and instrument of the kingdom of God.

Religious teaching

Over the centuries, the church has split into many denominations. The eastern Orthodox and western Roman Catholic churches separated in 1054. The 16th-century Reformation saw the Protestant Lutherans leave the Catholic Church. There was further fragmentation when Protestants divided into Baptists (who reject infant baptism), Congregationalists (whose individual congregations are autonomous), Presbyterians (who are governed by assemblies of church elders); and others.

All contemporary Christian denominations, however, claim that they too, like the early Christian community, adhere closely to the teaching of the apostles. Despite their many differences, they all share the basic belief that Jesus was the Messiah; that he performed God's work on earth, preaching, teaching and healing the sick; that he was crucified and buried, and then raised from the dead; that he ascended to the Father and that it is through him that people's sins are forgiven.

Worship, sacraments and fellowship

The church not only administers the sacraments. It is itself a sacrament. A 'sacrament' is a visible sign of God's grace. Christians believe that through the church people make contact with the risen Jesus, who exists today in the members of his church. Thus, the church is a sign of the presence of the risen Christ. Its role is to make present Jesus' mediation and the gifts of the Holy Spirit, so that Christians might live perfectly in one family as the children of God. It does this primarily through public worship and the administration of the sacraments.

In the Roman Catholic Church and many Orthodox churches there are seven sacraments (baptism, confirmation, the Eucharist, penance, anointing of the sick, ordination, and matrimony). Protestants recognise only two (baptism and the Eucharist) or in some Lutheran churches, three (baptism, confession and the Eucharist). Partaking in the sacraments of the church, accepting its doctrines and following an appropriate way of life lead believers into a 'fellowship', a special relationship with God through Jesus Christ, and with each other.

The sharing of possessions is not compulsory in modern Christian communities, but some denominations have religious orders made up of monks or nuns who live, work and pray together and hold everything in common. Others practise tithing, where members agree to give one tenth of their income towards the church's work. All denominations do what they can to assist the sick and the poor.

Mission, service and outreach

The Christian church is not only a *sign* of God's grace. It is an *instrument* of God's grace as well. It works for peace, charity, fair trade, gender equality, overseas mission, etc., to bring about the justice and mercy that God intends for all creation. It is the agent of God's mission to the world.

It responds to natural disasters such as famine, epidemics and earthquakes and man-made crises such as wars and acts of terrorism, giving tangible support to survivors. It is committed to helping refugees to resettle and rebuild their lives. It has programmes for health and child development in poor, third world countries. It seeks to give vulnerable communities access to basic necessities such as clean water, and empowers them to realise their economic potential by teaching simple agricultural methods and making small loans. It maintains several initiatives to foster peace in dangerous conflict zones, and attempts to establish harmony between hostile communities.

Attempts to get the world-wide church to respond as one on global peace and justice issues have been more successful than those aimed at developing a common approach to faith and order.

The global church has had more success in speaking with one voice on peace and justice issues than in reconciling doctrinal differences.

Acts 2: 46 reads: 'And the Lord added to their number daily those who were being saved'. This clearly demonstrates that although the commission for all believers (Matthew 28: 18–20) was to 'baptise all nations', that is, evangelise, it is also evident that the lifestyle of the New Testament community of believers was in itself a form of 'outreach' and many believed because of their actions and not just the message that they brought.

AO1 Activity

In order to see how the contemporary church is modelled on those actions of the early church it would be useful to draw a table that compares them as follows and complete the second column from the AO1 text in the book and any other evidence that you can collate:

Features of the New Testament community of believers as depicted in Acts 2:42–47	The contemporary church in providing worship and sacraments, religious teaching, mission, service and outreach, and fellowship for the community of believers
Devotion to Apostles' teaching	
Fellowship	
Breaking of bread	
Devotion to prayers	
Outreach / adding to their number	
Sold and gave to those in need	
Had all things in common	

Key quote

There is no real religious experience that does not express itself in charity. (C.H. Dodd)

Key quote

They devoted themselves to the apostles' teaching and to fellowship, to the breaking of bread and to prayer. Everyone was filled with awe at the many wonders and signs performed by the apostles. All the believers were together and had everything in common. They sold property and possessions to give to anyone who had need. Every day they continued to meet together in the temple courts. They broke bread in their homes and ate together with glad and sincere hearts, praising God and enjoying the favour of all the people. And the Lord added to their number daily those who were being saved. (Acts 2:42–47)

Key skills

Knowledge involves:

Selection of a range of (thorough) accurate and relevant information that is directly related to the specific demands of the question.

This means you choose the correct information relevant to the question set NOT the topic area. You will have to think and focus on selecting key information and NOT writing everything you know about the topic area.

Understanding involves:

Explanation that is extensive, demonstrating depth and/or breadth with excellent use of evidence and examples including (where appropriate) thorough and accurate supporting use of sacred texts, sources of wisdom and specialist language.

This means that you demonstrate that you understand something by being able to illustrate and expand your points through examples/supporting evidence in a personal way and NOT repeat chunks from a text book (known as rote learning).

Further application of skills:

Go through the topic areas in this section and create some bullet lists of key points from key areas. For each one, provide further elaboration and explanation through the use of evidence and examples.

AO1 Developing skills

It is now time to reflect upon the information that has been covered so far. It is also important to consider how what you have learned can be focused and used for examination-style answers by practising the skills associated with AO1.

Assessment objective 1 (AO1) involves demonstrating knowledge and understanding. The terms 'knowledge' and 'understanding' are obvious but it is crucial to be familiar with how certain skills demonstrate these terms, and also, how the performance of these skills is measured (see generic band descriptors Band 5 for AS AO1).

▶ **Your new task is this:** below is a below average answer that has been written in response to a question requiring an examination of the importance of the New Testament community of believers. It is obviously a below average answer and so would be about band 2. It will be useful, initially, to consider what is missing from the answer and what is inaccurate. This time there is no accompanying list to assist you. In analysing the answer's weaknesses, in a group, decide upon five points that you would use to improve the answer in order to make it stronger. Then write out your additions, each one in a clear paragraph, remembering the principles of explaining with evidence and/or examples.

Answer

The key quote here is that 'they devoted themselves to the apostles' teaching and fellowship, to the breaking of bread and the prayers'. They also shared everything.

The apostles' teaching was proclaimed in the early church. It followed a particular pattern: that Jesus was the promised Messiah, that he died to save humankind, was resurrected on the third day and will come again.

The phrase 'breaking of bread' signifies the breaking of the bread at the Lord's Supper, the sacrament that Jesus himself had established as his memorial rite. It was a sacrament reflecting the members' communion with each other and with God.

Early Christians adhered to the traditional Jewish pattern of prayer. They prayed in the Temple at least three times a day. They also had 'all things in common', although it seems that this experiment failed.

Issues for analysis and evaluation

Whether the main role of the church is to provide religious teaching

This section covers AO2 content and skills

Specification content
Whether the main role of the church is to provide religious teaching.

The Christian church is sometimes criticised for being more concerned with its teaching – its dogma and doctrines – than it is with people.

The church has always been concerned with the correct interpretation of Scripture, and the fact that different people have interpreted Scripture in different ways has led to its fragmentation, much to the bewilderment of ordinary Christians.

In Jesus' teaching, the commandment to love people comes second to the commandment to love God. Love for people is simply a way for Christians to show their love to God who loved them enough to give them his Son as their Saviour.

This means accepting the church's doctrine about the saving work of Jesus achieved through his life, death and resurrection. In other words, it is the doctrine that gives rise to the love for people. The church's main role is to provide the doctrine.

Thus the church is accused of loving people only with a view to making them Christians. Moreover, some of its traditional teaching (e.g. on the ordination of women, birth control, marriage of divorced or gay people, etc.) seems to be insensitive.

An opposing argument is that the church has always sought to help those in need. It takes as its example Jesus' great emphasis on caring for the weak, the poor, the suffering, the marginalised, the vulnerable.

Contemporary Christianity puts love for people into practice through encouraging fair trade, charity work, the pursuit of peace, care for the environment, etc. Churches of different denominations often find ways of working together on humanitarian projects and lobbying on behalf of the underprivileged.

For many Christians, this is far more important than doctrine, and follows the key teaching of Jesus not simply about refraining from activities that hurt another but for positive action that benefits another.

True Christian love (*agape*) is unselfish and unconditional and is not directed at making converts.

However, it does all depend, in one sense, upon what one means by religious teaching. The Christian Gospel is pro-active and an inherent imperative within the teachings of Jesus and Paul is to act in a Christian manner. As Paul says in 1 Corinthians 4:17–18, 'therefore I urge you to imitate me … Timothy, my son whom I love … will remind you of my way of life in Christ Jesus, which agrees with what I teach everywhere in every church'. There is a strong argument, therefore, to suggest that the teachings of the Christian church are essential but only in so far as they deliver a message that is life-changing and impacts upon the poor and needy and those who suffer in both spiritual and physical terms.

In conclusion, one possible solution could be that providing religious teaching is very important but only in the sense that this religious teaching needs to be listened to and acted upon. Religious teaching that is delivered and has no visible impact upon the lives of others is no business of the church.

AO2 Activity *Possible lines of argument*

Listed below are some conclusions that could be drawn from the AO2 reasoning in the above text:

1. The church's main role is to provide religious teaching.

2. The church's main role is to care for the underprivileged.

3. The church has a role both to provide religious teaching and to care for the underprivileged.

Consider each of the conclusions drawn above and collect evidence and examples to support each argument from the AO1 and AO2 material studied in this section. Select one conclusion that you think is most convincing and explain why it is so. Now contrast this with the weakest conclusion in the list, justifying your argument with clear reasoning and evidence.

Specification content

The extent to which contemporary Christian churches should follow the New Testament model.

The extent to which contemporary Christian churches should follow the New Testament model

In some respects, the New Testament church provides an excellent model for contemporary Christian churches.

The early Christian community in Jerusalem had several srengths. It was apparently united in belief, practices, worship and communal life. It operated under the divine guidance of the Holy Spirit. Its apostles, particularly Peter, spoke with authority, were able to perform miracles and gave strong leadership.

Its life was founded on prayer. It was mission orientated – its goal was to persuade followers of the Jewish religion to be baptised and to accept Jesus as the promised Messiah.

It was effectively administered, and made immediate arrangements to settle disagreements.

It was joyful, enthusiastic and effective, and obviously appealed to outsiders.

In other respects, however, the model is somewhat flawed.

The New Testament church also had several weaknesses. The story of the early Christian community in Jerusalem records evidence of disobedience, love of money, lying to the Holy Spirit, favouritism and jealousy.

Its leadership was inconsistent, fluctuating between the theocratic and sometimes autocratic, with occasional elements of democratic participation.

Moreover, it does not appear initially to have made any attempt to convert anyone outside the Jewish community. When that eventually happened, mostly through Paul's mission, it led to the first threat of a split within Christianity between Gentiles and Jews. There was a period of bitter argument between Paul and the Judaizers.

There is an argument, therefore, that to see the New Testament model as a 'Golden Age' of Christianity is possibly to glorify matters. What seems to be important is that in looking at the New Testament model of the early church, it is not seen as the perfect and complete example.

Lessons are to be learned from the mistakes and confusions experienced by the early church as depicted in the New Testament. The incidents of Ananias and Sapphira in Acts 5 and the debate in Acts 15 between the Council of Jerusalem and Paul are classic examples.

Indeed, if it were just Acts, then maybe we could be forgiven for seeing the New Testament model of the early church as an ideal, despite these problems. However, the fact is that the letters of Paul are full of his frustrations with the early church as it spread. For example, the church in Corinth was far from perfect: Paul writes in 1 Corinthians 1:5, 'some from Chloe's household have informed me that there are quarrels among you'. Again in 1 Corinthians 3:1, 'I could not address you as people who live by the Spirit but as people who are still worldly'. As the letter develops, Paul refers to 'arrogant' members, 'sexual immorality', 'boasting', 'lawsuits' and a general lack of discipline. This inspired Paul to write some of his greatest words concerning 'love' in 1 Corinthians 13. There is equally a strong polemic against the legalistic interpretation of Christianity by church in Rome in his letter to the Romans which N.T. Wright refers to as 'neither a systematic theology nor a summary of Paul's lifework, but it is by common consent his masterpiece'.

In conclusion, although there is much to admire about the New Testament model of the early church, there is obviously also much to learn from mistakes made. One could conclude that to put such a model on a pedestal would be unwise. Indeed, is there anywhere in the New Testament that implies that there is an actual model of the early church?

AO2 Activity *Possible lines of argument*

Listed below are some conclusions that could be drawn from the AO2 reasoning in the above text:

1. The New Testament church is an excellent model for contemporary Christians.
2. The New Testament church is a flawed model for contemporary Christians.
3. The New Testament church had some good points that contemporary Christians should follow.

Consider each of the conclusions drawn above and collect evidence and examples to support each argument from the AO1 and AO2 material studied in this section. Select one conclusion that you think is most convincing and explain why it is so. Now contrast this with the weakest conclusion in the list, justifying your argument with clear reasoning and evidence.

AO2 Developing skills

It is now time to reflect upon the information that has been covered so far. It is also important to consider how what you have learned can be focused and used for examination-style answers by practising the skills associated with AO2.

Assessment objective 2 (AO2) involves 'analysis' and 'evaluation'. The terms may be obvious but it is crucial to be familiar with how certain skills demonstrate these terms, and also, how the performance of these skills is measured (see generic band descriptors Band 5 for AS AO2).

Obviously, an answer is placed within an appropriate band descriptor depending upon how well the answer performs, ranging from excellent, good, satisfactory, basic/limited to very limited.

▶ **Your new task is this:** below is a below average answer that has been written in response to a question requiring an evaluation of the contention that the contemporary Christian church is more of an instrument than a sign of God's grace. It is obviously a below average answer and so would be about band 2. It will be useful, initially, to consider what is missing from the answer and what is inaccurate. This time there is no accompanying list to assist you. In analysing the answer's weaknesses, in a group, decide upon five points that you would use to improve the answer in order to make it stronger. Then write out your additions, each one in a clear paragraph. Remember, it is how you use the points that is the most important factor. Apply the principles of evaluation by making sure that you: identify issues clearly; present accurate views of others, making sure that you comment on the views presented; reach an overall personal judgement. You may add more of your own suggestions, but try to negotiate as a group and prioritise the most important things to add.

Answer

You could argue that the Christian church is a sign of God's grace because it administers the sacraments, of which there are seven in all. However, not many people receive the sacraments today.

The church is more relevant as an instrument of God's grace. This is when it works on behalf of God for peace, charity, fair trade, gender equality, overseas mission, etc.

A key quote comes from Dodd: 'There is no real religious experience that does not express itself in charity.'

Attempts to get the world-wide church to respond as one on global peace and justice issues have been more successful than those aimed at developing a common approach to the sacraments, particularly the Eucharist.

Key skills

Analysis involves identifying issues raised by the materials in the AO1, together with those identified in the AO2 section, and presents sustained and clear views, either of scholars or from a personal perspective ready for evaluation.

This means that it picks out key things to debate and the lines of argument presented by others or a personal point of view.

Evaluation involves considering the various implications of the issues raised based upon the evidence gleaned from analysis and provides an extensive detailed argument with a clear conclusion.

This means that the answer weighs up the various and different lines of argument analysed through individual commentary and response and arrives at a conclusion through a clear process of reasoning.

Specification content

Selected key moral principles of
Christianity.

Key term

Moral principle: the basis of right
and wrong

---

quickpire

3.11 On what are Christian moral
principles based?

C: Key moral principles

Make sure that you have read and understood the set texts:

Leviticus 19:34; Luke 10:25–28

Exodus 34:6–7; 1 John 4:19–21

1 Samuel 12:24; Ephesians 4:25–27

2 Corinthians 1:12; 1 Timothy 1:5

Matthew 6:14–15; Colossians 3:12–13

An introduction to Christian key moral principles

Christian moral principles are based on God's laws regarding behaviour. Christians
attempt to obey certain rules laid down by God and recorded in Old Testament law
and in the New Testament teaching of Jesus.

Study tip

Make sure that you know the Bible teachings on which different Christian moral
principles are based. The band descriptor for AO1 (Level 5) expects 'Thorough
and accurate reference made to sacred texts and sources of wisdom, where
appropriate'.

Jesus was often challenged by Jewish leaders about his attitude to Old Testament
law, and why his followers did not adhere to it more closely. He was once asked
by a Pharisee, a member of a sect devoted to the study of the law, 'Teacher, which
commandment in the law is the greatest?' Jesus replied: '"You shall love the Lord
your God with all your heart, and with all your soul, and with all your mind." This
is the greatest and first commandment. And a second is like it: "You shall love
your neighbour as yourself." On these commandments hang all the law and the
prophets.'

Key quote

[Jesus] said … : 'You shall love the Lord your God with all your heart, and
with all your soul, and with all your mind.' This is the greatest and first
commandment. And a second is like it: 'You shall love your neighbour
as yourself'. On these commandments hang all the law and the prophets.
(Matthew 22:37–40)

Moses receiving the Ten Commandments

Love of neighbour

When he commanded his followers to 'love the Lord your God with all your heart, and with all your soul, and with all your mind', Jesus was echoing what had already been written in the Old Testament Book of Deuteronomy (6:5): 'You shall love the Lord your God with all your heart, and with all your soul and with all your might'.

When he commanded his followers to 'love your neighbour as yourself', he was echoing the Old Testament Book of Leviticus (19:18). Leviticus goes on to give a reason for this commandment: the Israelites are to welcome foreigners as fellow citizens and to 'love the alien as yourself, for you were aliens in the land of Egypt' (19:34).

Specification content

Selected key moral principles of Christianity: the importance of love of neighbour (Leviticus 19:34; Luke 10:25–28).

The two commandments are repeated in the introduction to one of Jesus' best known parables, the parable of the Good Samaritan (Luke 10:25–37). When asked by a lawyer: 'What must I do to inherit eternal life?', Jesus replies: 'What is written in the law'. The lawyer answers that the law commands people to love God and to love their neighbour as themselves. 'That's right,' says Jesus. 'Do this and you will live'. The lawyer then asks: 'And who is my neighbour?' Jesus replies by telling the story of a man who is attacked and robbed on the road from Jerusalem to Jericho. Two Jewish religious leaders pass him by without offering assistance, but a Samaritan (and the Jews considered Samaritans to be their enemies) stops, binds his wounds and takes care of him. He then commands the lawyer: 'Go and do likewise'.

It is obvious that for Jesus one's 'neighbour' is not simply the person who happens to live next door, but everyone whom we happen to meet on life's journey, friend or enemy. In the Sermon on the Mount, Jesus told his followers that they had heard the old saying, 'Love your neighbour and hate your enemy'. 'But', he went on, 'I tell you: Love your enemies and pray for those who persecute you' (Matthew 5:43). To love God with heart, soul and mind is to recognise that everyone is part of his creation. They deserve respect, and their needs and desires must be as highly regarded as one's own. This is a Christian imperative.

The Good Samaritan

Specification content

Selected key moral principles of
Christianity: God's love as a potential
model for Christian behaviour
(Exodus 34:6–7; 1 John 4:19–21).

Key quote

The Lord passed before him and proclaimed, 'The Lord, the Lord, a God merciful and gracious, slow to anger, and abounding in steadfast love and faithfulness, keeping steadfast love for the thousandth generation, forgiving iniquity and transgression and sin, yet by no means clearing the guilty, but visiting the iniquity of the parents upon the children and the children's children, to the third and fourth generation.' (Exodus 34:6–7)

quickfire

3.12 Why, according to the First Epistle of John, must Christians love God?

Specification content

Selected key moral principles of
Christianity: regard for truth (1
Samuel 12:24; Ephesians 4:25–27).

God's love as a potential model for Christian behaviour

The basic model for Christian behaviour is the love shown for human beings by God himself. In both the Old and New Testaments, God is presented as a God of love.

In the Old Testament, in Exodus 34:6–7, there is a famous passage where God reveals himself to Moses and, in words attributed to God himself, describes his own character, proclaiming that he is:

Moses Seeing God

- *Merciful*: he does not punish us as we deserve;
- *Gracious*: he gives us what we do not deserve;
- *Slow to anger*: he is longsuffering, patient;
- *Abounding in steadfast love and faithfulness*: his love and faithfulness are unchanging;
- *Keeping steadfast love for the thousandth generation*: his is an active love for the entire human race;
- *Forgiving iniquity, and transgression and sin*: he forgives all – iniquity (our fallen nature), transgression (deliberate and defiant revolt against his law) and sin (every wrong we do, accidental or otherwise);
- *Yet by no means clearing the guilty*: he is nevertheless a God of justice; his love includes correction; those who insist on doing evil will be punished;
- *Visiting the iniquity of the parents upon the children, and upon the children's children, to the third and the fourth generation*: the consequence of sin is likely to be felt by the family of the guilty, but will be limited to three or four generations.

The New Testament teaches that God's steadfast love and faithfulness was revealed fully in the life, and particularly in the death, of Jesus. Since God has so loved human beings, human beings must so love God. In his First Epistle (4:19–21), John insists that it is impossible to love God without also loving other people. Those who say that they love God, and hate their brothers and sisters, are liars. If they do not love their brothers or sisters, whom they have seen, how can they love God, whom they have not seen? True love of God includes a love of humanity.

A regard for truth

Christians have always considered themselves to be guardians of the truth. By 'truth' they mean the ultimate meaning and value of existence. They believe that the Bible communicates the truth about the nature of God, the Person of Jesus, the history of salvation.

In the Old Testament (1 Samuel 12:24), the Israelites are commanded to 'fear the Lord, and serve him faithfully with all your heart; for consider what great things he has done for you'.

The 'great things' he had done for Israel was to free her from captivity in Egypt and lead her through forty years in the wilderness to the promised land of Canaan. In recognition of this, the Israelites are called 'to serve him faithfully'.

The New Testament account of God's saving grace is even more dramatic. Through the death and resurrection of Jesus he has freed human beings from captivity to sin and death and led them to a promised eternal life. In recognition of this, Christians are called to put away their old, corrupt self and to clothe themselves with 'the new self, created according to the likeness of God in true righteousness and holiness' (Ephesians 4:24). Paul advises Christians to 'speak the truth to our neighbours, for we are members of one another. Be angry but do not sin; do not let the sun go down on your anger, and do not make room for the devil' (Ephesians 4:25–27).

It is all right, says Paul, for Christians to feel angry. But their anger must be directed against sin, and it must not be allowed to fester in the heart because that opens the door for the devil.

The role of conscience

The Bible teaches that human beings, because they are made in the image of God, have an innate sense of right and wrong. They are able to view life situations in a moral or ethical light and to judge that some actions are 'right' and others 'wrong'. This ability is called 'conscience'. As Paul writes in his First Letter to Timothy (1:5), 'the aim of such instruction is love that comes from a pure heart, a good conscience, and sincere faith'.

Christians believe that their conscience is informed both by the Bible and the work of the Holy Spirit. When they violate the standards that they believe are expected of them, they experience guilt. They are then to confess their sin and experience God's forgiveness.

If conscience is repeatedly ignored, one's sensitivity to moral issues becomes desensitised, and one goes along with things one knows to be wrong.

Conscience can also become overly sensitive, condemning the believer for normal human failures, and leading to false guilt. The Christian's goal is to develop a mature conscience based on biblical teaching as illuminated by the Holy Spirit. The Bible is clear that believers must have their conscience informed by God's word.

Christians must therefore satisfy themselves that their moral behaviour satisfies their conscience and will not cause guilt.

The need for forgiveness

Forgiveness is a prominent theme in the teaching of Jesus. In his Sermon on the Mount (Matthew 6:14–5), he told his followers that if they do not forgive, they themselves will not be forgiven. It is this idea that lies behind the petition in the Lord's Prayer, 'And forgive us our debts, as we also have forgiven our debtors' (Matthew 6:12).

On another occasion, when Peter asked him 'how often should I forgive? As many as seven times?', Jesus answered: 'Not seven times, but I tell you, seventy-seven times' (Matthew 18:21–22). The answer suggests that forgiveness is not easy. People who have been wronged do not naturally overflow with grace and mercy. Nevertheless, Christians must spend a lifetime forgiving.

Paul echoes Jesus' teaching. For him, the model for Christian forgiveness is the forgiveness freely granted to sinners by God. In his Letter to the Colossians (3:12–13), he writes 'Bear with one another and, if anyone has a complaint against another, forgive each other; just as the Lord has forgiven you, so you also must forgive'.

Forgiveness is therefore a conscious choice that Christians must make through a decision of the will motivated by obedience to God. They believe that forgiveness sets them free from all feelings of anger and hurt that previously constrained them.

AO1 Activity

Draw up a table identifying the biblical sources for Christian moral principles.

Specification content

Selected key moral principles of Christianity: the role of conscience (2 Corinthians 1:12; 1 Timothy 1:5).

Key quote

Indeed, this is our boast, the testimony of our conscience: we have behaved in the world with frankness and godly sincerity, not by earthly wisdom but by the grace of God – and all the more toward you. (2 Corinthians 1:12)

quickfire

3.13 What two things inform the Christian conscience?

Specification content

Selected key moral principles of Christianity: the need for forgiveness (Matthew 6:14–15; Colossians 3:12–13).

Key quote

For if you forgive others their trespasses, your heavenly Father will also forgive you; but if you do not forgive others, neither will your Father forgive your trespasses. (Matthew 6:14–15)

quickfire

3.14 How many times did Jesus say his followers should forgive those who had wronged them?

quickfire

3.15 What, according to Paul, is the model for Christian forgiveness?

Key skills

Knowledge involves:

Selection of a range of (thorough) accurate and relevant information that is directly related to the specific demands of the question.

This means you choose the correct information relevant to the question set NOT the topic area. You will have to think and focus on selecting key information and NOT writing everything you know about the topic area.

Understanding involves:

Explanation that is extensive, demonstrating depth and/or breadth with excellent use of evidence and examples including (where appropriate) thorough and accurate supporting use of sacred texts, sources of wisdom and specialist language.

This means that you demonstrate that you understand something by being able to illustrate and expand your points through examples/supporting evidence in a personal way and NOT repeat chunks from a text book (known as rote learning).

Further application of skills:

Go through the topic areas in this section and create some bullet lists of key points from key areas. For each one, provide further elaboration and explanation through the use of evidence and examples.

AO1 Developing skills

It is now time to reflect upon the information that has been covered so far. It is also important to consider how what you have learned can be focused and used for examination-style answers by practising the skills associated with AO1. Assessment objective 1 (AO1) involves demonstrating knowledge and understanding. The terms 'knowledge' and 'understanding' are obvious but it is crucial to be familiar with how certain skills demonstrate these terms, and also, how the performance of these skills is measured (see generic band descriptors Band 5 for AS AO1).

▶ **Your new task is this:** below is a list of several key points bulleted in response to a question requiring an examination of how the Bible helps Christians to make moral decisions. It is obviously a very full list. It will be useful, initially, to consider what you think are the most important points to use in planning an answer. This exercise, in essence, is like writing your own set of possible answers that are listed in a typical mark scheme as indicative content. In a group, select the most important points you feel should be included in a list of indicative content for this question. You will need to decide upon two things: which points to select; and then, in which order to put them in an answer.

List of indicative content:

- Christian moral behaviour must reflect the character of God.
- In the Book of Exodus, God describes his own character to Moses. He is:
  - *Merciful*
  - *Gracious*
  - *Slow to anger*
  - *Abounding in steadfast love and faithfulness*
  - *Keeping steadfast love for the thousandth generation*
  - *Forgiving iniquity, and transgression and sin*
  - *Yet by no means clearing the guilty*
  - *Visiting the iniquity of the parents upon the children, and upon the children's children, to the third and the fourth generation: the consequence of sin will be limited to three or four generations.*
- The New Testament teaches that God's steadfast love and faithfulness was revealed fully in the life, and particularly in the death, of Jesus.
- Christians must base their moral decisions on Christ's teachings.
- Christians must base their moral decisions on God's love.
- Christians must first love God.
- It is impossible to love God without also loving other people. True love of God includes a love of humanity.
- Christians must love whoever they happen to meet on life's journey. They must do so to reflect their own experience of the love of God.
- They must be guardians of the Christian truth, which is that God is a saving God who has freed human beings from captivity to sin and death and led them to a promised eternal life. In recognition of this, Christian anger must be directed not against sinners but against sin, and it must not be allowed to fester in the heart.
- Christians believe that human beings, because they are made in the image of God, have an innate sense of right and wrong. This ability is called 'conscience'.
- Christians believe that their conscience is informed both by the Bible and the work of the Holy Spirit.
- Christians must satisfy themselves that their moral behaviour satisfies their conscience and will not cause guilt.
- Christians must show forgiveness.
- The model for Christian forgiveness is the forgiveness freely granted to sinners by God.

Issues for analysis and evaluation

Whether love of neighbour is the most important moral principle in Christianity

All Christians would agree that the love of neighbour is a very important moral principle. It is a principle that Jesus not only taught and illustrated in his parables but also demonstrated by example during his life on earth in the assistance he gave to the suffering and the bereaved and the sympathy he showed to the marginalised and those in need. Jesus once said: 'In everything do to others as you would have them do to you; for this is the law ...' (Matthew 7:12). This Golden Rule sums up his ethical teaching.

In addition, the importance of love of neighbour can be seen in other writings in the New Testament. The classic example is in 1 Corinthians 13 where Paul declares that 'these three remain: faith, hope and love. But the greatest of these is love'. The same word agape is used. Alternatively, 1 John 2:10 states, 'Anyone who loves their brother and sister lives in the light, and there is nothing in them to make them stumble'.

However, there are many important moral principles in Christianity such as care for the poor and needy, those who are oppressed and those who suffer. The imperative to give to those less fortunate than others is also important as is the guidance offered by the Ten Commandments. The issue is, can Christians really perform the above without 'love of neighbour'? The answer appears to be 'no'. Love for neighbour, it could be argued, drives other moral principles.

It could be argued that Jesus' followers are called to love all God's people. In so doing, they not only make the world a better place but they also find their own fulfilment. To be loved, they must love. To be respected, they must respect all people. To be forgiven, they must forgive. If they wish not to be judged, they must not judge others.

In addition, Jesus wanted his followers to reject selfishness and seek the welfare of their fellow human beings, whoever and wherever they may be. This universal love is at the very heart of his teaching. Thus, his followers believe that to practise this love is the work that God has given them to do on earth.

Another argument that is put forward, however, is that in Jesus' teaching, the love of neighbour comes second to the love of God. The first 'moral' imperative is to 'love the Lord your God with all your heart, and with all your soul, and with all your mind'. How can this be 'moral', one asks? This argument states that Christians believe that the difficult task of loving their neighbour is not something that they can do by themselves; it can only be done when they are united to God in love. Thus, the true love of neighbour cannot be accomplished without loving God.

Therefore, it is impossible to love all people in all their imperfections unless one is united in love to the God who created them as his children. Equally, it is impossible to be united in love to God without loving the men and women that he has created. For Christians, loving God is made visible in a sacrificial loving of others. In this sense, love for neighbour is transformed into the supreme moral imperative for Christians.

In conclusion, it could be argued that all moral principles in Christianity emanate from the love for God and are expressed initially through an imperative to 'love your neighbour', but also extends to other moral principles of Christian life. In this sense, love of neighbour is the most important moral principle in Christianity in so far as it reflects the love for, and of, God.

This section covers AO2 content and skills

Specification content
Whether love of neighbour is the most important moral principle in Christianity.

AO2 Activity *Possible lines of argument*

Listed below are some conclusions that could be drawn from the AO2 reasoning in the above text:

1. The love of neighbour is the most important moral principle in Christianity.
2. The love of God is the most important moral principle in Christianity.
3. The love of God and the love of neighbour are inseparable in Christianity.

Consider each of the conclusions drawn above and collect evidence and examples to support each argument from the AO1 and AO2 material studied in this section. Select one conclusion that you think is most convincing and explain why it is so. Now contrast this with the weakest conclusion in the list, justifying your argument with clear reasoning and evidence.

Specification content

The extent to which God's behaviour towards humans is the basis for Christian morality.

The extent to which God's behaviour towards humans is the basis for Christian morality

Christians often base their morality on what they know of God and his behaviour towards human beings. In Exodus 34, God revealed himself to Moses as merciful and gracious, long-suffering and patient, active in his love for Israel, forgiving and just. The Old Testament depicts God's relationship with the Israelites as one of loving faithfulness (Hebrew chesed).

In addition to this, God's behaviour towards human beings can be seen in the legal directives of the Torah in terms of the treatment of strangers in Leviticus 19:34 'The foreigner residing among you must be treated as your native-born. Love them as yourself, for you were foreigners in Egypt. I am the Lord your God.' In addition, the basis of Jesus' 'Greatest Commandment' is found in Leviticus 19:18, 'Do not seek revenge or bear a grudge against anyone among your people, but love your neighbour as yourself. I am the Lord.'

Also, Christians believe that these attributes of God were fully revealed in the New Testament in the life, and particularly in the death, of Jesus. As John 3:16 puts it, 'God so loved the world that he gave his only Son, so that everyone who believes in him may not perish but may have eternal life.'

In addition to this, since God has so loved human beings, human beings must so love God. True love of God includes a love of humanity. As John says in his First Epistle, 'we love because he first loved us'. The appropriate way to respond to God's love is therefore to show love for human beings by keeping his commandments. 'The love of God is this,' says John, (1 John 5:3), 'that we obey his commandments. And his commandments are not burdensome'.

The commandments, however, include not only the Ten Commandments given to the Israelites through Moses, but Jesus' interpretation of them and, in particular, those issued by Jesus himself during his earthly life. The example of God, in the form of Jesus, is of paramount significance.

In Jesus, it could be argued that we see the exemplary model of unconditional and sacrificial love. As Jesus was fully God then the actions he performed must become the basis for Christian morality. He accepted all, forgave the sinners, welcomed the outcasts and cared for the weak and sick.

Indeed, some Christians would say that all that matters is trying to live and treat others as Jesus did. But it is not easy always to follow Jesus' example and teachings. After all, Jesus challenged his followers to leave home and possessions and 'take up their cross'. Very few people have responded in full to this challenge.

Nevertheless, with the assistance of the Holy Spirit, as demonstrated explicitly in Acts, Christians aim to live a life that is shaped by the message of the Gospel and transformed by the love of God so that they may act as a force for good in the world, advocating the rights of all people to peace and social justice.

In conclusion, Christian morality could be argued to be directly and explicitly influenced by God's behaviour towards humans.

AO2 Activity *Possible lines of argument*

Listed below are some conclusions that could be drawn from the AO2 reasoning in the above text:

1. The basis for Christian morality is God's behaviour towards humans.

2. The basis for Christian morality is the Ten Commandments.

3. The basis for Christian morality is the example and teachings of Jesus.

4. The basis for Christian morality includes all of these things.

Consider each of the conclusions drawn above and collect evidence and examples to support each argument from the AO1 and AO2 material studied in this section. Select one conclusion that you think is most convincing and explain why it is so. Now contrast this with the weakest conclusion in the list, justifying your argument with clear reasoning and evidence.

AO2 Developing skills

It is now time to reflect upon the information that has been covered so far. It is also important to consider how what you have learned can be focused and used for examination-style answers by practising the skills associated with AO2.

Assessment objective 2 (AO2) involves 'analysis' and 'evaluation'. The terms may be obvious but it is crucial to be familiar with how certain skills demonstrate these terms, and also, how the performance of these skills is measured (see generic band descriptors Band 5 for AS AO2).

Obviously an answer is placed within an appropriate band descriptor depending upon how well the answer performs, ranging from excellent, good, satisfactory, basic/limited to very limited.

▶ **Your new task is this:** below is a list of several key points bulleted in response to a question requiring an evaluation of whether or not Jesus' teachings concerning key moral principles are the basis of Christian morality. It is obviously a very full list. It will be useful, initially, to consider what you think are the most important points to use in planning an answer. This exercise, in essence, is like writing your own set of possible answers that are listed in a typical mark scheme as indicative content. In a group, select the most important points you feel should be included in a list of indicative content for this question. You will need to decide upon two things: which points to select; and then, in which order to put them in an answer.

List of indicative content:

In support

- It should be, because Jesus' teaching is the teaching of God.
- In the Sermon on the Mount, Jesus instructed his followers to adopt his interpretation of God's law.
- Many of Jesus' parables and actions illustrate the basis for moral behaviour.
- Some Christians would say that all that matters is trying to live and treat others as Jesus did.
- As it is not always easy to follow Jesus' example and teachings, Jesus has sent down the Holy Spirit to assist people in their efforts.
- With the assistance of the Holy Spirit, Christians aim to live a holy life.
- Their aim is to act as a force for good in the world.

Challenges

- The basic template for Christian morality is the Mosaic law.
- In the Sermon on the Mount, Jesus insisted that he had not come to abolish the Mosaic law but to fulfill it.
- Jesus also insisted that the first commandment was to love God.
- Christians therefore often base their morality on what they know of God and his behaviour towards humans.
- Thus, they too must be merciful, gracious, long-suffering, patient, active in love for humanity, forgiving and just.
- Christians believe that these attributes of God were fully revealed in the life, and particularly in the death, of Jesus.
- Christians therefore love God because God first loved them.
- True love of God includes a love of humanity.
- The appropriate way to respond to God's love is therefore to show love for human beings.

Key skills

Analysis involves identifying issues raised by the materials in the AO1, together with those identified in the AO2 section, and presents sustained and clear views, either of scholars or from a personal perspective ready for evaluation.

This means that it picks out key things to debate and the lines of argument presented by others or a personal point of view.

Evaluation involves considering the various implications of the issues raised based upon the evidence gleaned from analysis and provides an extensive detailed argument with a clear conclusion.

This means that the answer weighs up the various and different lines of argument analysed through individual commentary and response and arrives at a conclusion through a clear process of reasoning.

This section covers AO1 content and skills

Specification content

The case for infant baptism by Augustine and Zwingli (the role of baptism in salvation; the role and importance of Christian parents).

quickfire

4.1 What, according to traditional doctrine, does baptism remove?

Key term

Circumcision: a Jewish religious rite performed on male infants on the eighth day after birth to commemorate God's covenant with Abraham (Genesis 17)

quickfire

4.2 According to Augustine, who began the practice of infant baptism?

A: Religious identity through diversity in baptism

The case for infant baptism

Most Christian denominations regard the practice of baptising infants as a traditional custom. Augustine wrote that it was a 'tradition received from the apostles' as a means of removing original sin. The Council of Carthage in 418 CE declared that 'even babies, who are yet unable to commit any sin personally, are truly baptised for the forgiveness of sins, for the purpose of cleansing by rebirth what they have received by birth'.

There is New Testament support for the practice:

- Luke 18:15–16: 'People were bringing even infants to him that he might touch them; ... Jesus called for them and said, "Let the little children come to me, and do not stop them; for it is to such as these that the kingdom of God belongs".' The only way that the Bible gives of bringing anyone to Jesus is through baptism.

- In John 3:5, Jesus tells Nicodemus: 'I tell you, no one can enter the kingdom of God without being born of water and Spirit'. His words include infants.

- In his Great Commission (Matthew 28:19), Jesus commands his disciples to go 'and make disciples of all nations, baptising them in the name of the Father and of the Son and of the Holy Spirit'. Infants are not excluded.

- Acts 2:38–39: Peter said to them, 'Repent, and be baptised every one of you in the name of Jesus Christ so that your sins may be forgiven; and you will receive the gift of the Holy Spirit. For the promise is for you, for your children.'

- The apostles baptised whole 'households' (Acts 16:33; 1 Cor. 1:16). The term indicates a family as a unit, including children and infants.

- In I Corinthians 7:14, Paul writes that one believing parent in a household makes the children 'holy'.

- Baptism is the Christian equivalent of the Jewish rite of circumcision, 'a spiritual circumcision' (Colossians 2:11–12). Christians are 'buried with' Jesus in baptism and 'raised with him through faith in the power of God'. Circumcision, however, does not save. Baptism does.

Infant baptism appears to have been uniformly practised in the early church, and was supported by all the church Fathers – Irenaeus, Hippolytus, Origen, Cyprian, Gregory of Nazianz, John Chrysostom and Augustine.

Augustine wrote extensively on baptism. Infant baptism, he maintained, was something that the universal church had 'always held', and was 'most correctly believed to have been handed down by apostolic authority'.

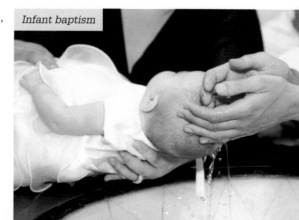
Infant baptism

Augustine believed that baptised infants, who are not yet able to imitate Christ, are 'ingrafted' into his body. Christ gives to believers the grace of his Spirit, 'which he secretly infuses even into infants'.

The fact that infants are not able to profess personal faith does not prevent the church from baptising them. According to Augustine, 'When children are presented to be given spiritual grace, it is not so much those holding them in their arms who present them ... as the whole company of saints and faithful Christians .... It is done by the whole of Mother Church'. Infants who are baptised believe not on their own account, but 'through the Church's faith communicated to them'.

For Augustine, baptism is a sacrament – a religious rite that imparts spiritual grace. He wrote that the North African Christians of his time called the sacrament of baptism 'salvation' and the sacrament of the Eucharist 'life', and supposed that this derived from apostolic tradition, which asserted that 'without baptism and participation at the table of our Lord, it is impossible for anyone to attain either to the kingdom of God or to salvation and life eternal'. He concluded that 'the sacrament of baptism is most assuredly the sacrament of regeneration'.

In 416 CE, the Council of Mileum II endorsed this teaching. Quoting Paul in Romans 5:12 ('sin came into the world through one man, and death came through sin, and so death spread to all because all have sinned'), the Council asserted that

'on account of this rule of faith, even infants, who in themselves thus far have not been able to commit any sin, are therefore truly baptised unto the remission of sins, so that that which they have contracted from generation may be cleansed in them by regeneration'.

This doctrine was constantly reaffirmed during the Middle Ages. Even amongst the early Reformers, there was no controversy on the subject. Huldrych Zwingli (1484–1531), the leader of the Protestant Reformation in Switzerland, differed only in that he regarded baptism not as the means of regeneration but as its sign and seal. Baptism, he wrote, 'cannot contribute in any way to the washing away of sins' Quoting Paul in Romans 4:11 (that Abraham 'received the sign of circumcision as a seal of the righteousness that he had by faith'), so baptism, according to Zwingli, seals the remission of sin by the blood of Christ, and our incorporation in Christ by faith, which is produced by the Holy Spirit. In infant baptism, the divine promise is guaranteed to young children on the basis of their parents' pledge to bring them up in the Christian faith. The sacrament is divinely instituted, and efficacious to aid and strengthen faith and to confer spiritual blessing. It is a sign of belonging to the new covenant, just as circumcision was a sign of belonging to the old.

Infant baptism is usually by aspersion. The water is sprinkled over the infant's head.

Huldrych Zwingli

Specification content

The case for believer's baptism with reference to Karl Barth (the example of Christ; importance of consent).

quickfire

4.4 What is the meaning of the derogatory term *Anabaptist*?

Key quotes

I have never taught Anabaptism … But the right baptism of Christ, which is preceded by teaching and oral confession of faith, I teach, and say that infant baptism is a robbery of the right baptism of Christ. (Hubmaier)

If any one saith, that little children, for that they have not actual faith, are not, after having received baptism, to be reckoned amongst the faithful; and that, for this cause, they are to be rebaptised when they have attained to years of discretion; or, that it is better that the baptism of such be omitted, than that, while not believing by their own act, they should be baptised in the faith alone of the Church; let him be anathema. (Council of Trent, Canon XIII, 1547)

An example of believers' baptism

The case for believers' baptism

No Christian objections to the practice of infant baptism were ever voiced until the Reformation, when a diverse group of radical reformers began baptising adults who had made a profession of their faith. Hated by both Catholics and Protestants alike, the name *Anabaptists*, meaning 'rebaptisers', was given them by their persecutors. The early members of the movement did not accept the name, arguing that their baptism was no 'second baptism' because infant baptism was unscriptural and therefore null and void.

There is New Testament support for believers' baptism. The New Testament has no record of infants being baptised. Baptism is administered only to adult believers old enough to decide for themselves:

- In Acts 8:12, the Samaritans are baptised after they believe the good news preached by Philip.
- In Acts 8:35–36, the Ethiopian eunuch is baptised after he believes.
- In Acts 9:18, the apostle Paul is baptised after he encounters Jesus in a vision on the road to Damascus.
- In Acts 10:44–48, Peter baptises Cornelius and his household after they show evidence of their faith.
- In Acts 16:14–15, Lydia and her household are baptised after she believes.
- In Acts 19:5–6, the disciples of John the Baptist are baptised after they accept Paul's teaching about Jesus.

Baptism invariably follows faith and is the first act of discipleship made by people of responsible age who have turned to Jesus from their sinful way of life.

However, as Anabaptist practice involved baptising believers who had already been baptised as infants, both Catholics and Protestants interpreted it as 'rebaptising', and in 1547 it was denounced by the Council of Trent.

Study tip

Go to www.churchinwales.org.uk and click on *Life* then *Baptism* to see what the contemporary church in Wales believes about baptism.

AO1 Activity

On a piece of plain A4 paper draw two parallel columns. Label the columns 'Infant Baptism' and 'Believers' Baptism'. As you go through this section add key points to the columns, using different colours. Then, on a piece of lined A4 paper, write out a report on the comparisons and contrasts between the two models of baptism.

Karl Barth: Baptism as union with Christ

Believers' baptism was endorsed by Karl Barth, one of the 20th century's most influential theologians. In a series of lectures later published in a book entitled *The Teaching of the Church regarding Baptism* (1948), Barth wrote that baptism does not bring about human salvation, but bears testimony to salvation by its symbolic representation of renewal in Christ.

Barth's argument may be summarised as follows:

- Baptism with water marks the first step of a life lived in Christ.

- It is a response to baptism in the Spirit – God's grace in converting individuals.

- It is not a sacrament, but rather a human action that acknowledges the one true sacrament, which is 'the sacrament of the history of Jesus Christ'. It is thus an image of salvation history. Its power resides in Christ.

- It 'seals' the reality of God's grace, but does not generate that reality.

- Because it is a human response to God's grace, it must be a free act. Since it is the beginning of a life of obedience to God, there can be no suggestion of coercion, for coercion undermines obedience.

- Infant baptism is misguided because it is coercive. While it is true, valid and effectual in an objective sense, it is deficient in the subjective sense that the individual baptised is not necessarily ready or willing to take the first step that it marks. In Barth's words, 'it is not done in obedience, it is not administered according to proper order, and therefore it is necessarily clouded baptism'.

Barth was aware that his views would cause controversy. In his foreword in 1967 to the last volume (IV:4) of his *Church Dogmatics*, which is on baptism, he foresaw that 'this book, which ... will be my last publication, will leave me in ... theological and ecclesiastical isolation ... I am thus to make a poor exit with it'. While some theologians, including Jürgen Moltmann, supported him, and some, such as T.P. Forsyth, argued that both infant and believers' baptism should be equally recognised, others took a more traditional stance:

- Oscar Cullmann (*Baptism in the New Testament*, 1950) objected that baptism signifies both death to sin and resurrection to the life of the Spirit. It is a passive reception of God's work and does not depend on the recipient's faith.

- Peter Brunner (*Worship in the Name of Jesus*, 1968) insisted that in baptism Christ unites people in his body, regardless of whether they are infant or adult.

- Others have emphasised that in baptism we receive what Christ has already done for us, unconditioned by anything in us.

Believers' baptism is usually by **immersion**, when the water covers the candidate's whole body.

Karl Barth

quickfire

4.5 What was Barth's main objection to infant baptism?

Key term

Immersion: baptising by immersing the candidate's whole body in water

Key skills

Knowledge involves:

Selection of a range of (thorough) accurate and relevant information that is directly related to the specific demands of the question.

This means you choose the correct information relevant to the question set NOT the topic area. You will have to think and focus on selecting key information and NOT writing everything you know about the topic area.

Understanding involves:

Explanation that is extensive, demonstrating depth and/or breadth with excellent use of evidence and examples including (where appropriate) thorough and accurate supporting use of sacred texts, sources of wisdom and specialist language.

This means that you demonstrate that you understand something by being able to illustrate and expand your points through examples/supporting evidence in a personal way and NOT repeat chunks from a text book (known as rote learning).

Further application of skills:

Go through the topic areas in this section and create some bullet lists of key points from key areas. For each one, provide further elaboration and explanation through the use of evidence and examples.

AO1 Developing skills

It is now time to reflect upon the information that has been covered so far. It is also important to consider how what you have learned can be focused and used for examination-style answers by practising the skills associated with AO1.

Assessment objective 1 (AO1) involves demonstrating knowledge and understanding. The terms 'knowledge' and 'understanding' are obvious but it is crucial to be familiar with how certain skills demonstrate these terms, and also, how the performance of these skills is measured (see generic band descriptors Band 5 for AS AO1).

▶ **Your new task is this:** below is a list of indicative content that could be used in response to a question requiring an examination of the case for believers' baptism. The problem is that it is not a very full list and needs completing! It will be useful, as a group, to consider what is missing from the list. You will need to add at least five points that you would use to improve the list and/or give more detail to each point that is already in the list. Then, as a group, agree on your final list and write out your new list of indicative content, remembering the principles of explaining with evidence and/or examples.

If you then put this list in order of how you would present the information in an essay, you will have your own plan for an ideal answer.

List of indicative content:

- The practice began when a group of radical reformers (nicknamed 'Anabaptists') began baptising adults who had made a profession of their faith.
- In the New Testament, baptism is administered only to adult believers old enough to decide for themselves.
- Baptism invariably follows faith and is the first act of discipleship made by people of responsible age who have turned to Jesus.
- Believers' baptism was endorsed by Karl Barth. Barth believed that baptism is not a sacrament, but rather an image of salvation history.
- For him, infant baptism is misguided because it is coercive.
- *Your added content*
- *Your added content*
- Etc.

Issues for analysis and evaluation

The criteria for expressing the commitment to be baptised

This section covers AO2 content and skills

Specification content

The criteria for expressing the commitment to be baptised.

Some Christians believe that the gift of baptism should be consciously accepted by the person who receives it; an infant is incapable of doing this.

The church, however, has always considered the baptism of infants a serious duty requiring faithful attention to church teaching and practice. Baptism is necessary for salvation. It is not only a sign of God's love; it also imparts that love. It frees recipients from original sin and gives them a share in the life of God.

While there is no reason why these blessings should not be gifted to infants, the true meaning of infant baptism cannot be fulfilled unless the church is assured that there is a readiness to nurture the gift by providing the infant with a continuing education in the Christian life. These assurances are usually given by the parents or close relatives. If the church feels that they are not serious, the sacrament can be delayed or even refused.

The role of the parents is crucial. It is very important that they receive appropriate instruction from a priest in preparation for the baptism and that they actively participate in the sacrament. They have priority over the godparents, although the godparents role in the child's education can sometimes be essential. The congregation too has a role in the child's Christian upbringing. Baptism is therefore never administered without faith, in this case the faith of the parents and that of the whole church.

Ideally, the church should agree to a request for infant baptism only if the parents can give a reasonable assurance that, once the child is baptised, it will receive a Christian upbringing.

As for those Christians who practise believer's baptism, they would argue that baptism is simply a symbol of having been saved and not a requirement for salvation. It is symbolic, not sacramental, a form of obedience to Jesus. They base their belief first on New Testament accounts which record that baptism always followed conversion, never preceded it, and second on the conviction that a commitment to follow Jesus should always be voluntary.

For these Christians, the principle of the priesthood of all believers means that any member of the local congregation may perform baptisms. Because it involves a public confession of faith, the rite is conducted, where possible, in a public place. These places include rivers, lakes and swimming pools, but more commonly specially built church baptisteries.

The timing of the baptism is not important, except that it must follow a person's conversion and profession of faith. Sometimes, candidates for baptism are required to attend classes for new Christians.

All adult believers who are baptised are expected to become a member of a local congregation. They become part of a community of believer-priests. In this respect, baptism represents a covenant between the person being baptised and a specific church congregation.

AO2 Activity *Possible lines of argument*

Listed below are some conclusions that could be drawn from the AO2 reasoning in the text:

1. The criteria for expressing a commitment to be baptised are flawed in the case of infant baptism.

2. The criteria for expressing a commitment to be baptised are flawed in the case of believers' baptism.

3. The criteria for expressing a commitment to be baptised are based on fundamentally different views of the meaning of baptism

Consider each of the conclusions drawn above and collect evidence and examples to support each argument from the AO1 and AO2 material studied in this section. Select one conclusion that you think is most convincing and explain why it is so. Now contrast this with the weakest conclusion in the list, justifying your argument with clear reasoning and evidence.

Specification content

The extent to which both infant and
adult baptism are just symbolic acts.

The extent to which both infant and adult baptism are just symbolic acts

Those who agree with the contention that both infant and adult baptism are just symbolic acts would argue that salvation begins when people repent of their sins and acknowledge Jesus as their Saviour. Baptism is not mandatory for salvation. Both the thief on the cross (Luke 23:42) and Saul (Acts 9:17–18) were saved before being baptised.

Baptism is a secondary and subsequent action to salvation. It is, nevertheless, rich in symbolism for many Christians. One understanding to support this view is that it is a symbol of the forgiveness that is already received. It is not the means of spiritual regeneration, but merely its sign and seal. Another argument is that it is a symbol that the recipient has been accepted into the Christian church. In addition to this, it is also seen as a symbol of belonging to the new covenant, just as circumcision was a symbol of belonging to the old. Finally, it is also seen as a symbol of the waters of the Flood, which divided between the lost and the saved.

More importantly for some, it is a symbol of the recipient's participation in the death, burial and resurrection of Jesus – the recipient passes through a watery 'death' to a resurrected 'life'. Whilst this can be seen as purely symbolic, some see this as more of an empowering experience akin to a sacrament.

Indeed, those who disagree with the contention would argue that while baptism most certainly does have symbolic aspects, it is not primarily a symbol. It is primarily a sacrament, a rite that imparts God's grace. It is the first phase of salvation. The second phase is a faithful partaking of the Eucharist.

Baptism, for many, has the primary purpose of washing away original sin and it imparts the gift of the Holy Spirit. The recipient's soul is profoundly changed by the experience of baptism that cannot be explained away through symbolic interpretation alone. Theologians call this an ontological change. An ontological change is a change in the nature of someone's existence. The baptised person is 'a new creation' according to Paul in 2 Corinthians 5:17, 'Therefore, if anyone is in Christ, the new creation has come: The old has gone, the new is here!'

Indeed, it could be argued that baptism unites the recipient with Jesus. Paul writes that 'in the one Spirit we were all baptised into one body' (1 Corinthians 12:13). Later, in 1 Corinthians 12:27 he makes clear that he is referring to 'the body of Christ'.

Baptism also serves the purpose and function of uniting the recipient with the church. Paul identifies Christ's body with Christ's church in 1 Corinthians 12:28, 'Now you are the body of Christ, and each one of you is a part of it.' Thus, people do not just 'join' the church as they join, say, the local tennis club; they are incorporated into the church, Christ's body, by baptism.

In conclusion, it is clear that there is much symbolism associated with the act of baptism. However, it is also clear that for many it is much more than this, ranging from unification with Christ and Christ's body the church to an individual ontological change in the person baptised.

AO2 Activity *Possible lines of argument*

Listed below are some conclusions that could be drawn from the AO2 reasoning in the above text:

1. Both infant and adult baptism are merely symbolic acts.

2. Both infant and adult baptism are sacraments.

3. Both infant and adult baptism are both sacraments and symbolic acts.

Consider each of the conclusions drawn above and collect evidence and examples to support each argument from the AO1 and AO2 material studied in this section. Select one conclusion that you think is most convincing and explain why it is so. Now contrast this with the weakest conclusion in the list, justifying your argument with clear reasoning and evidence.

AO2 Developing skills

It is now time to reflect upon the information that has been covered so far. It is also important to consider how what you have learned can be focused and used for examination-style answers by practising the skills associated with AO2.

Assessment objective 2 (AO2) involves 'analysis' and 'evaluation'. The terms may be obvious but it is crucial to be familiar with how certain skills demonstrate these terms, and also, how the performance of these skills is measured (see generic band descriptors Band 5 for AS AO2).

Obviously, an answer is placed within an appropriate band descriptor depending upon how well the answer performs, ranging from excellent, good, satisfactory, basic/limited to very limited.

▶ **Your new task is this:** below is a list of indicative content that could be used in response to a question requiring an evaluation of whether the baptism administered today by most mainstream churches is biblical. The problem is that it is not a very full list and needs completing! It will be useful, as a group, to consider what is missing from the list. You will need to add at least six points (three in support and three against) that you would use to improve the list and/or give more detail to each point that is already in the list. Remember, it is how you use the points that is the most important factor. Apply the principles of evaluation by making sure that you: identify issues clearly; present accurate views of others, making sure that you comment on the views presented; reach an overall personal judgement. You may add more of your own suggestions, but try to negotiate as a group and prioritise the most important things to add.

Then, as a group, agree on your final list and write out your new list of indicative content, remembering the principles of explaining with evidence and/or examples. If you then put this list in order of how you would present the information in an essay, you will have your own plan for an ideal answer.

List of indicative content:

In support

- In Luke, Jesus says: 'Let the little children come to me, and do not stop them'. The only way that the Bible gives of bringing anyone to Jesus is through baptism.
- In his Great Commission (Matthew 28:19), Jesus commands his disciples to go 'and make disciples of all nations, baptising them in the name of the Father and of the Son and of the Holy Spirit'. Infants are not excluded.
- The apostles baptised whole 'households', including children and infants.
- *Your added content*
- *Your added content*
- Etc.

Against

- The New Testament has no record of infants being baptised.
- The apostle Paul is baptised after he encounters Jesus in a vision on the road to Damascus.
- Lydia and her household are baptised after she believes.
- *Your added content*
- *Your added content*
- Etc.

Key skills

Analysis involves identifying issues raised by the materials in the AO1, together with those identified in the AO2 section, and presents sustained and clear views, either of scholars or from a personal perspective ready for evaluation.

This means that it picks out key things to debate and the lines of argument presented by others or a personal point of view.

Evaluation involves considering the various implications of the issues raised based upon the evidence gleaned from analysis and provides an extensive detailed argument with a clear conclusion.

This means that the answer weighs up the various and different lines of argument analysed through individual commentary and response and arrives at a conclusion through a clear process of reasoning.

Specification content

The importance of the Eucharist
in the life of contemporary
Christian communities; the
similarities in Eucharistic practice
in Christian traditions.

quicKpire

4.6 What is the meaning of the word *Eucharist*?

Key quote

For I received from the Lord what I also handed on to you, that the Lord Jesus on the night when he was betrayed took a loaf of bread, and when he had given thanks, he broke it and said, 'This is my body that is for you. Do this in remembrance of me.' In the same way he took the cup also, after supper, saying, 'This cup is the new covenant in my blood. Do this, as often as you drink it, in remembrance of me.' For as often as you eat this bread and drink this cup, you proclaim the Lord's death until he comes. (1 Corinthians 11:23–27)

Specification content

Selected modern Roman Catholic
theories (transignification and
transfinalization).

Key quote

His body and blood are truly contained in the sacrament ..., the bread and wine having been transubstantiated, by God's power, into his body and blood. (The Fourth Lateran Council, 1215)

B: Religious identity through diversity in Eucharist

The importance of the Eucharist in contemporary Christian communities

The Eucharist is the Christian church's most important sacrament. The word *Eucharist* is the Greek word for 'thanksgiving'. Other names for the Eucharist are Holy Communion, Mass and the Lord's Supper.

Aware of his approaching death on the cross, Jesus shared a farewell meal with his disciples (see Matthew 26:26–30 and parallels). He took ordinary bread and wine and shared them, saying of the bread, 'This is my body', and of the wine, 'This is my blood'. According to Paul (1 Corinthians 11: 26) , he then added, 'For as often as you eat this bread and drink the cup, you proclaim the Lord's death until he comes'.

Similarities in Eucharistic practice in Christian traditions

Ever since, Christians have taken bread and wine to remember Jesus and to give thanks for him. They believe that, by the grace of God, the bread and wine are symbols of, or in some cases, become, Jesus' body and blood. Just as human bodies need physical sustenance, so do human souls need spiritual sustenance. In the mystical, timeless sustenance of the Eucharist, Christians believe that Jesus is present with them.

The Eucharist is therefore the physical re-enactment of Jesus' Last Supper with his disciples. It is also:

- a meal which has the real presence of Jesus;
- a source of grace to which all believers are invited;
- a memorial of Jesus' last hours on earth;
- a celebration of Jesus' resurrection, and of the Christian's life with him;
- a symbolic reminder of God's love for humankind;
- a fellowship, or 'communion' of Christians and between them and God.

The Roman Catholic understanding of the Eucharist

Transubstantiation

From the earliest times, it appears that Christians believed that the bread and the wine of the Eucharist, when consecrated by an ordained priest, changed into the actual body and blood of Jesus. Since the 11th century, the Roman Catholic Church has used the term **transubstantiation** to describe this change.

Study tip

This section is full of new terms. In revising, instead of just drawing up a glossary of Key terms try changing this into a flowchart that links each understanding of the Eucharist. This will show an ability to present their inter-relatedness and demonstrate 'extensive depth and/or breadth' (AO1 band 5 descriptor).

The Orthodox Church position is similar, but it prefers to use terms such as 'trans-elementation'or 're-ordination', and considers the change a 'divine mystery'. What Orthodox Christians consume is 'mysteriously' the body and blood of Christ, not 'real' human flesh and blood.

The Roman Catholic doctrine was challenged by Protestant Reformers, but in 1551 it was reaffirmed by the Council of Trent as 'that wonderful and singular conversion of the whole substance of the bread into the Body, and of the whole substance of the wine into the Blood … which conversion indeed the Catholic Church most aptly calls Transubstantiation'.

It was again reaffirmed in 1965 in Pope Paul VI's encyclical, *Mysterium Fidei* (The Mystery of the Faith) written in response to two new terms proposed by two contemporary Catholic theologians, *transignification* and *transfinalization*.

Transignification

Transignification is a theory put forward by Edward Schillebeeckx (1914–2009). It proposes that when the priest consecrates the bread and wine of the Eucharist they take on the real significance of Christ's body and blood, but are not chemically changed. Christ is therefore sacramentally, but not physically, present.

The theory draws on two concepts which have to do with psychological reality:

- That all effective signs consist of two parts – 'signifier' and 'signified'. In the Eucharist, the 'signifier' is the substance of the bread and the wine, while the 'signified' is the substance of Christ's body and blood.
- That there are two kinds of presence, local and personal. Pupils may be 'locally present' in a class, but if their thoughts are far away, then they are not 'personally present'. In the Eucharist Jesus is personally, but not locally present.

Transfinalization

Transfinalization is a theory put forward by the German Jesuit theologian, Karl Rahner (1904–1984).

It proposes that when the priest consecrates the bread and wine of the Eucharist their purpose and finality are changed, but not their substance. They do not become Christ's body and blood, but serve a new function, which is to stir up faith in the mystery of Christ's redemptive love.

Both theories are concerned more with the meaning of the Eucharist than with its substance, and both were condemned by Pope Paul VI in the encyclical *Mysterium Fidei* (1965), because they can be understood as denying transubstantiation.

Key quote

… it is not permissible to … discuss the mystery of transubstantiation without mentioning what the Council of Trent had to say about the marvellous conversion of the whole substance of the bread into the Body and the whole substance of the wine into the Blood of Christ, as if they involve nothing more than 'transignification' or 'transfinalization' as they call it … the spread of these and similar opinions does great harm to belief in and devotion to the Eucharist.
(Pope Paul VI, *Mysterium Fidei*, 1965)

quickfire

4.7 Define what is meant by *transubstantiation*.

Eucharist/Mass in a Roman Catholic church

Key terms

Transfinalization: the belief that when the bread and wine are consecrated their purpose is changed, but not their substance

Transignification: the belief that Christ is sacramentally, but not physically, present in the consecrated bread and wine

Transubstantiation: the belief that the bread and wine of the Eucharist actually become the body and blood of Christ when consecrated by a priest

Specification content
Selected Protestant approaches
(consubstantiation and
memorialism).

quickfire

4.8 Define what is meant by
consubstantiation.

Key quote

Of the Supper of the Lord they (i.e.
the Lutheran churches) teach that
the Body and Blood of Christ are
truly present, and are distributed
to those who eat the Supper of the
Lord; and they reject those that
teach otherwise. (Article X, The
Augsburg Confession, 1530)

quickfire

4.9 Whose view of the Eucharist does the
term *memorialism* describe?

Key terms

Consubstantiation: the belief that
the body and blood of Christ co-exist
with the consecrated bread and wine
of the Eucharist

Memorialism: the belief that the
consecrated bread and wine of
the Eucharist are merely symbolic
representations of Christ's body and
blood

Predestination: the belief that God
has elected some people to be saved,
but not others

Virtualism: the belief that Christ's
unique power (Latin *virtus*) is present
in the consecrated bread and wine, but
that this power is received only by the
predestined elect

Protestant understandings of the Eucharist

Consubstantiation

The term **consubstantiation** has been used in the English language since the late
16th century to describe a doctrine put forward by Protestant Reformers in that
century to challenge the Roman Catholic doctrine of transubstantiation.

It teaches that the bread and wine of the Eucharist do not change into the actual
body and blood of Christ when consecrated by a priest. They remain bread and
wine. Nevertheless, Christ is spiritually present 'with them, in them and under
them'. The bread 'co-exists' with his body and the wine with his blood.

The prefix *trans-* means 'across, over'. So *trans*ubstantiation means that the
substance of the bread and wine literally *change over* to become the body and blood
of Jesus. The prefix *con-* means 'with'. So *con*substantiation means that the body
and blood of Jesus *co-exist with* the substance of the bread and wine.

The term is often employed to designate the view of the Eucharist held by Martin
Luther (1483–1546), the Father of the Protestant Reformation, but it was never
used by him and is rejected by most Lutheran churches as unbiblical. While it is
true that Luther asserted the 'real presence' of Jesus in the bread and the wine, the
term he used was not 'consubstantiation' but 'sacramental union'. The doctrine
was set out in the Lutheran Augsburg Confession of 1530.

Memorialism

Memorialism is a term used to describe the view of the Eucharist held by
Huldrych Zwingli (1484–1531). Zwingli denied the real presence of Christ in the
sacrament and taught that the bread and wine do not communicate him to the
recipient. They are rather symbolic representations of his body and blood. In Luke
22:19, Jesus commands
his followers to 'Do this in
remembrance of me'. The
Eucharist is therefore a
commemorative ceremony
where participants
remember Jesus' sacrifice
for them on the cross. Jesus
is present in the sacrament
only to the degree that each
individual brings him and
his work to mind.

John Calvin

Virtualism

Virtualism is a term used to describe the view of the Eucharist associated with John Calvin (1509–1564). Calvin taught the doctrine of **predestination**, which asserted that God, even before he created the world, had chosen some people, whom Calvin called 'the elect', to receive salvation, while the rest were left to continue in their sins and receive eternal damnation.

Calvin's view of the Eucharist arose from this belief. He taught that Christ's body cannot be present in the Eucharist, because Christ's body has ascended into Heaven (Acts 1:9–11). He did not, however, deny the presence of Christ's unique power (Latin *virtus*) in the bread and wine, but believed that this power is received only by the elect, who have been predestined to receive salvation. For this reason, the doctrine of virtualism is also known as 'receptionism'.

Study tip

One of the best ways of experiencing how different Christian traditions celebrate the Eucharist is to attend an Eucharistic service at various denominations.

AO1 Activity

Prepare a brief courtroom case to defend the doctrine of consubstantiation against that of transubstantiation. The accused (defendant) is a Protestant Reformer and his legal representative must outline how the doctrine of consubstantiation fits in with Christian theology. The case for the prosecution will be advised by the Roman Catholic Church and will accuse the defendant of holding dangerous and heretical views that challenge the sacredness of the Eucharist.

This exercise will help you in selecting the key, relevant information for an answer to a question on Catholic and Protestant understandings of the Eucharist and also form a basis for some AO2 evaluation.

quickfire

4.10 Give two terms used to describe Calvin's view of the Eucharist.

Key quote

And he took bread, gave thanks and broke it, and gave it to them, saying, 'This is my body given for you; do this in remembrance of me.' In the same way, after the supper he took the cup, saying, 'This cup is the new covenant in my blood, which is poured out for you.' (Luke 22:19–20)

Key skills

Knowledge involves:

Selection of a range of (thorough) accurate and relevant information that is directly related to the specific demands of the question.

This means you choose the correct information relevant to the question set NOT the topic area. You will have to think and focus on selecting key information and NOT writing everything you know about the topic area.

Understanding involves:

Explanation that is extensive, demonstrating depth and/or breadth with excellent use of evidence and examples including (where appropriate) thorough and accurate supporting use of sacred texts, sources of wisdom and specialist language.

This means that you demonstrate that you understand something by being able to illustrate and expand your points through examples/supporting evidence in a personal way and NOT repeat chunks from a text book (known as rote learning).

Further application of skills:

Go through the topic areas in this section and create some bullet lists of key points from key areas. For each one, provide further elaboration and explanation through the use of evidence and examples.

AO1 Developing skills

It is now time to reflect upon the information that has been covered so far. It is also important to consider how what you have learned can be focused and used for examination-style answers by practising the skills associated with AO1.

Assessment objective 1 (AO1) involves demonstrating knowledge and understanding. The terms 'knowledge' and 'understanding' are obvious but it is crucial to be familiar with how certain skills demonstrate these terms, and also, how the performance of these skills is measured (see generic band descriptors Band 5 for AS AO1).

You are now nearing the end of this section of the course. From now on the task will have only instructions with no examples; however, using the skills you have developed in completing the earlier tasks, you should be able to apply what you have learned to do and complete this successfully.

▶ **Your new task is this:** you will have to write a response under timed conditions to a question requiring an examination of the different doctrines of the Eucharist that you have studied. You will need to focus for this and apply the skills that you have developed so far:

> **1. Begin with a list of indicative content. Perhaps discuss this as a group. It does not need to be in any order.**

> **2. Develop the list using examples.**

> **3. Now consider in which order you would like to explain the information.**

> **4. Then write out your plan, under timed conditions, remembering the principles of explaining with evidence and/ or examples.**

Use this technique as revision for each of the topic areas that you have studied. The basic technique of planning answers helps even when time is short and you cannot complete every essay.

Issues for analysis and evaluation

The extent to which there is any common ground within contemporary understandings of the Eucharist

There is much common ground within contemporary understandings of the Eucharist. All Christians, whatever their denomination, would agree on several basic principles. They would all agree that the Eucharist was instituted by Jesus as a re-enactment of his Last Supper with his disciples. It is a meal in which the bread and the wine signify the body and blood of Jesus. As such, it is a source of grace to which all believers are invited.

They would all agree that it is a memorial of Jesus' last hours on earth. It is also a celebration of Jesus' resurrection, and of the Christian's life with him. It is, therefore, a symbolic reminder of God's love for humankind, and also a fellowship, or 'communion' of Christians and between them and God.

However, Christians still disagree on what happens to the bread and wine when they are consecrated. The official Roman Catholic position is that they are changed into the actual body and blood of Christ (*transubstantiation*). The Orthodox position is similar (*divine mystery*).

The official position of the Lutheran Church is that the substance of the bread and the wine do not change, but that Christ is spiritually present 'with them, in them and under them'. This is traditionally known as *consubstantiation*, although Luther's own term for it was *sacramental union*.

Other Reformed churches follow Zwingli's teaching that Christ is only present in the bread and the wine to the extent that the recipient brings him and his work to mind (*memorialism*), or that of Calvin, which is that Christ's power is received only by the elect through faith. Some contemporary Roman Catholic theologians have proposed other theories, e.g. Schillebeeckx (*transignification*) and Rahner (*transfinalization*), but have been criticised by the Pope.

Despite this it is clear that all Christians have taken bread and wine to remember Jesus and to give thanks for him. All Christians who partake in the Eucharist believe that, by the grace of God, the bread and wine are symbols of, or in some cases, become, Jesus' body and blood. As has been noted earlier, in the mystical, timeless sustenance of the Eucharist, Christians believe that Jesus is present with them. It is clear that the common elements are more significant than, and override, any differences in understanding. Such universal elements include an acknowledgement of the real presence of Jesus, offered to all believers in memory of Jesus' final hours, his death and resurrection, and, a reminder of God's love in a Christian's life and in fellowship, or 'communion' with other Christians. Such common features, it could be argued, are the most important.

This section covers AO2 content and skills

Specification content
The extent to which there is any common ground within contemporary understandings of the Eucharist.

AO2 Activity *Possible lines of argument*

Listed below are some conclusions that could be drawn from the AO2 reasoning in the above text:

1. There is much common ground within contemporary understandings of the Eucharist.
2. There is little common ground within contemporary understandings of the Eucharist.
3. There is some common ground within contemporary understandings of the Eucharist.

Consider each of the conclusions drawn above and collect evidence and examples to support each argument from the AO1 and AO2 material studied in this section. Select one conclusion that you think is most convincing and explain why it is so. Now contrast this with the weakest conclusion in the list, justifying your argument with clear reasoning and evidence.

Specification content

The extent to which theoretical beliefs about the Eucharist affect the practice of different denominations.

The extent to which theoretical beliefs about the Eucharist affect the practice of different denominations

On first glance, it might appear that the celebration of the Eucharist in denominations that believe in transubstantiation is far more dignified than in denominations that do not.

In the Orthodox and Roman Catholic traditions, the Eucharist is the central point of worship. It is celebrated every Sunday and on feast days with the greatest possible pomp and ceremony – ornate vessels, colourful vestments, dignified music and liturgy, processions, incense, and a formal structure.

The Orthodox Divine Liturgy consists of three parts: the *Liturgy of Preparation*, said only by the priest and deacon, when the the bread and wine are prepared; the *Liturgy of the Catechumens*, which is public and includes several Litanies, hymns, a reading from the Epistles and the Gospels and a homily; the *Liturgy of the Faithful*, which is restricted to baptised persons and includes the Eucharistic prayer (the *anaphora*), the *epiklesis* (calling down the Holy Spirit on the elements), the Lord's Prayer and the taking of communion.

The Roman Catholic Mass consists of four parts: *An Introductory* Rite (blessing, penitence, Gloria); the *Liturgy of the Word* (biblical readings, homily, creed); the *Liturgy of the Eucharist* (preparation of the bread and wine, Eucharistic prayer, the Lord's Prayer, a sign of peace, the breaking of the bread, the taking of communion); a *Concluding Rite* (blessing and dismissal).

However, the Eucharist is equally the central point of worship in churches that believe in the 'real presence' (e.g. Lutheran and Anglican). These churches too celebrate it frequently with appropriate ceremony and structure.

Calvinist churches may celebrate the Eucharist less frequently, perhaps once a month, but the custom has a devotional basis, which is to give people adequate time to reflect on their state of sin.

In churches with a memorialist view of the Eucharist, celebration may be even less frequent and may lack ceremony and a formal liturgy and structure, but is nevertheless conducted in a prayerful, dignified manner. Most congregations reserve a period of time for self-examination and private, silent confession just before partaking of communion.

In conclusion, it may be said that while churches that believe in transubstantiation may treat the consecrated bread and wine with exceptional pomp and ceremony, the Eucharist is celebrated with great devotion in all Christian traditions.

In this sense, theoretical beliefs about the Eucharist affect the practice of different denominations in a wide variety of ways, reflecting the depth and complexity in understanding of the physical act itself. Indeed, this is cause for celebration rather than division and once again highlights the richness and mystery of the Eucharist.

However, the reverse side of this argument is to point out the fact that whilst this is clearly the case, the substance of the Eucharist remains the same always in that the re-enactment of the last supper and Jesus' body and blood as bread and wine are the absolute foundation.

AO2 Activity Possible lines of argument

Listed below are some conclusions that could be drawn from the AO2 reasoning in the above text:

1. Theoretical beliefs about the Eucharist profoundly affect the practice of different denominations.

2. Theoretical beliefs about the Eucharist partly affect the practice of different denominations.

3. Theoretical beliefs about the Eucharist have no bearing on the devotion with which it is celebrated in different denominations.

Consider each of the conclusions drawn above and collect evidence and examples to support each argument from the AO1 and AO2 material studied in this section. Select one conclusion that you think is most convincing and explain why it is so. Now contrast this with the weakest conclusion in the list, justifying your argument with clear reasoning and evidence.

AO2 Developing skills

It is now time to reflect upon the information that has been covered so far. It is also important to consider how what you have learned can be focused and used for examination-style answers by practising the skills associated with AO2.

Assessment objective 2 (AO2) involves 'analysis' and 'evaluation'. The terms may be obvious but it is crucial to be familiar with how certain skills demonstrate these terms, and also, how the performance of these skills are measured (see generic band descriptors Band 5 for AS AO2).

Obviously an answer is placed within an appropriate band descriptor depending upon how well the answer performs, ranging from excellent, good, satisfactory, basic/limited to very limited.

You are now nearing the end of this section of the course. From now on the task will have only instructions with no examples; however, using the skills you have developed in completing the earlier tasks, you should be able to apply what you have learned to do and complete this successfully.

▶ **Your new task is this:** you will have to write a response under timed conditions to a question requiring an evaluation of whether or not there is a single correct way of celebrating the Eucharist. You will need to focus for this and apply the skills that you have developed so far:

> **1. Begin with a list of indicative content. Perhaps discuss this as a group. It does not need to be in any order. Remember, this is evaluation, so you need different lines of argument. The easiest way is to use the 'support' and 'against' headings.**

> **2. Develop the list using examples.**

> **3. Now consider in which order you would like to explain the information.**

> **4. Then write out your plan, under timed conditions, remembering to apply the principles of evaluation by making sure that you: identify issues clearly; present accurate views of others making sure that you comment on the views presented; reach an overall personal judgement.**

Use this technique as revision for each of the topic areas that you have studied. The basic technique of planning answers helps even when time is short and you cannot complete every essay.

Key skills

Analysis involves identifying issues raised by the materials in the AO1, together with those identified in the AO2 section, and presents sustained and clear views, either of scholars or from a personal perspective ready for evaluation.

This means that it picks out key things to debate and the lines of argument presented by others or a personal point of view.

Evaluation involves considering the various implications of the issues raised based upon the evidence gleaned from analysis and provides an extensive detailed argument with a clear conclusion.

This means that the answer weighs up the various and different lines of argument analysed through individual commentary and response and arrives at a conclusion through a clear process of reasoning.

Specification content

Christmas The similarities (with reference to the focus on incarnation of Christ) and differences (date of celebration; focus of Advent season; Christmas services) between the Eastern Orthodox and the Western churches' celebration of Christmas.

Key terms

Advent: in the Western Christian calendar the four weeks leading up to Christmas

Gaudete Sunday: the third Sunday of Advent

Parousia: the Second Coming of Christ

Saturnalia: an ancient Roman mid-winter festival in honour of the god, Saturn

The Nativity Fast: what corresponds to Advent in the Eastern Orthodox Church

quickfire

4.11 What two events do Western Christians anticipate during Advent?

C: Religious identity through diversity in festivals

Christmas

The English word *Christmas* is derived from the words 'Christ's Mass'. It is the celebration of the birth of Jesus.

AO1 Activity

As you read through this section, draw up a table of key aspects of Advent and Christmas with the columns entitled: 'Western rituals and their significance' and 'Eastern rituals and their significance'.

Advent in the Western church

No one knows the exact date of Jesus' birth. In Western Christianity, it is always celebrated on 25 December. It has been suggested that the early Christians chose this date to replace the Roman winter **saturnalia**, a festival that lasted from 17 to 23 December, and particularly the Roman winter solstice festival of *Dies Natalis Solis Invicti* (the 'Birthday of the Unconquered Sun'). Some of the symbols associated with Christmas are pagan in origin, e.g. the custom of lighting candles anticipates the return of sunlight and the cutting of evergreen trees for decorations illustrates the triumph of life over darkness and death.

In the Western church, Christmas is preceded by four weeks of preparation known as the season of **Advent** (from the Latin word *adventus* = coming). Advent is the beginning of the Western church year. It allows Christians to anticipate two events:

- The celebration of Jesus' First Coming to earth as a baby boy.
- Jesus' Second Coming at the end of time; the technical term for this is the *parousia*. The theme of the biblical readings and hymns during Advent is often preparation for the *parousia*.

The liturgical colour (the colour used for church hangings and clergy vestments) during Advent is traditionally violet or purple, although blue, representing hope, is becoming increasingly popular in Protestant churches. On the Third Sunday of Advent, known as *Gaudete Sunday*, a rose colour may be used. *Gaudete* is a Latin word meaning 'Rejoice'.

An Advent wreath

Advent customs include:

- An advent wreath, usually kept in church, but sometimes at home. The wreath has four candles (three purple and one rose-coloured) inserted around its edge, one for each of the four Sundays in Advent, and one white candle in the middle. The first candle represents hope; the second represents the prophets; the third, which is rose-coloured to match the liturgical colour for *Gaudete* Sunday, represents joy; the fourth, known as the Angel Candle, represents the Annunciation. The fifth candle is known as the Christ Candle and is lit during the Christmas Eve service.

- An advent calendar, first used by German Lutherans in the 19th and 20th centuries, but now widely popular, is a special calendar for each day of December up to and including Christmas Eve. The calendar windows for each day open to reveal an item relevant to the preparation for Christmas – a biblical verse, a poem, a prayer, or a small gift such as a chocolate or a toy.
- Christmas decorations are often set up in homes at the beginning of Advent.
- The traditional expectation that Christians should fast during Advent has now been relaxed in the Western church, but the season is still kept as a season of penitence.
- From 17 to 23 December, the Great Advent 'O Antiphons' may be sung at Evening Prayer each day. Each antiphon calls upon one of the attributes of Jesus mentioned in the Bible ('O Wisdom', 'O Lord', 'O Root of Jesse', 'O Key of David', 'O Dayspring', 'O King of the nations', 'O Emmanuel'). They form the basis for the popular Advent hymn, 'O come, O come, Emmanuel'.

Christmas in the Western church

During the period leading up to Christmas, churches will often hold carol services which relate the Christmas story in words and music. Often they will have a nativity crib depicting the stable at Bethlehem where Jesus was born. Nativity plays are also popular.

An old tradition in Wales is that of the *Plygain*. The word *plygain* comes from the Latin words *pulli cantio* = cockcrow. The *Plygain* was originally a carol service held in church between 3.00 and 6.00 on Christmas morning, when groups of men sang carols in the old metres to await the Eucharist at daybreak. Modern *Plygain* services are held on any weekday evening from the Feast of St Thomas' (21 December) to Old New Year's Day (13 January), and women too are now allowed to sing.

Christingle services have become popular in recent years. *Christingle* is a Scandinavian word meaning 'the light of Christ'. The christingle is an orange, into which four cocktail sticks bearing fruit or sweets are inserted. There is a red ribbon around the orange, and a small candle on top, which is lit during the service. The orange represents the world; the four cocktail sticks represent the four corners of the earth or the four seasons; the sweets and fruit represent the fruits of the earth; the light of the candle represents Jesus, the Light of the World; and the red ribbon represents his saving blood.

At Christmas itself, there are traditionally three Eucharists – the first at midnight on Christmas Eve, the second at dawn on Christmas morning and the third during Christmas Day.

Western Christians spend the rest of Christmas Day feasting and exchanging gifts with family and friends. The rampant consumerism which now characterises the feast is a fairly recent development, but is now threatening its religious observance.

A christingle

Key quote

Christmas is joy, religious joy,
an inner joy of light and peace.
(Pope Francis)

quickfire

4.12 What was the original *Plygain* tradition?

Key term

Plygain: originally an impromptu Welsh language service, held early on Christmas morning, when groups of men sang carols to await the Eucharist at daybreak

quickfire

4.13 On what date do many Orthodox Christians celebrate the birth of Christ?

Key quote

He has come, He Who by a single word called all things visible and invisible from non-existence into existence, Who by a word called into being birds, fishes, quadrupeds, insects, and all creatures, existing under His almighty providence and care; He has come … and in what humility has He come! He is born of a poor Virgin, in a cave, wrapped in poor swaddling clothes, and laid in a manger. Riches, honours, glory of this world! fall down, fall down in humility, tearful devotion, and deep gratitude before the Saviour of men, and share your riches with the poor and needy.

(St John of Kronstadt)

Advent in the Eastern church

Many Orthodox Christians celebrate Jesus' birth not on 25 December, as in the Western church, but on 7 January. This date corresponds to the old Julian calendar, that pre-dates the Gregorian calendar used in the West. The Armenian Orthodox Church uniquely celebrates Christmas on 6 January.

As in the Western church, the equivalent of the season of Advent is observed, but it is known in the Eastern church as the Nativity Fast. The Nativity Fast, which traditionally lasts for 40 days up to the Eve of the Nativity (6 January), entails abstaining from red meat, poultry, egg and dairy products, fish, oil and wine. The Eve of the Nativity is a strict fast day, known as *Paramony* ('preparation'), on which no solid food should be eaten until the first star appears in the evening sky.

The Nativity Fast does not begin the church year, as Advent does in the West, and there is no emphasis on the *parousia*. The liturgical colour red is used, with gold as an alternative. During the course of the Nativity Fast, a number of feast days celebrate Old Testament prophets who prophesied the incarnation. There are two other significant events:

- Two Sundays before the Nativity, the Sunday of the Forefathers commemorates the ancestors of the church.
- The Sunday before the Nativity, known as the Sunday of the Holy Fathers, commemorates all the righteous men and women who pleased God from the creation of the world up to Saint Joseph, husband of Jesus' mother, Mary.

Christmas in the Eastern church

On the Eve of the Nativity, the following services, which last all night, are held. They are intentionally parallel to those held on Good Friday, to illustrate the theological point that the purpose of the incarnation was to make possible the crucifixion and the resurrection:

- The Hours: special Psalms, hymns and biblical readings prescribed for each hour proclaim the joy and power of Christ's birth.
- Vespers: eight biblical readings celebrate the incarnation and show that Christ is the fulfillment of all prophecies.
- The Liturgy of St Basil the Great: in the past the baptismal liturgy at which catechumens were baptised and integrated into the Body of Christ.
- The Vigil, which begins with the Great Compline.
- Matins: now, for the first time, the words 'Christ is born' are sung while the congregation venerates an icon of the Nativity.

Christmas Day is a day for feasting and enjoying the company of family and friends. Candles may be lit to represent the light of Christ and the festive Christmas meal represents the end of fasting. White linen on dinner tables symbolises the cloth in which the baby Jesus was wrapped, and straw may be placed on the linen to symbolise the stable where he was born. Activity often depends on the country's culture and traditions. In some Orthodox cultures, people walk to seas, rivers and lakes as part of the Christmas Day liturgy and make holes in the frozen ice to bless the water. There is little emphasis on the sharing of gifts, and little of the consumerism that characterises the Western Christmas.

Study tip

One of the best ways of experiencing how different Christian traditions celebrate Christmas is to attend Christmas services at various denominations.

Easter

Easter is the most important of all Christian festivals. It is the celebration of the resurrection of Jesus.

Easter is a moveable feast. In most years, it is also celebrated on different dates in Western and Eastern Orthodox churches. This is because the churches disagree on how the calculation of the date of Easter is interpreted. There are two problems:

- While both churches agree on the formula for Easter ('the first Sunday after the first full moon on or after the vernal equinox'), they base the dates – as with the date of Christmas – on different calendars: Western churches use the Gregorian calendar; Orthodox churches use the older Julian calendar.

- They differ on the definition of the vernal equinox and the full moon. The Eastern church sets the date of Easter according to the actual, astronomical full moon and the actual equinox as observed along the meridian of Jerusalem, site of Jesus' crucifixion and resurrection. The Western church does not use the astronomically correct date for the vernal equinox, but a fixed date (March 21). And by full moon it does not mean the astronomical full moon but the 'ecclesiastical moon', which is based on tables created by the church. This allows the date of Easter to be calculated in advance rather than determined by actual astronomical observances.

- The Eastern Orthodox Church also applies the formula so that Easter always falls after the Jewish Passover, since the crucifixion and resurrection of Jesus took place after he entered Jerusalem to celebrate Passover. In the Western church, Easter sometimes precedes Passover by weeks.

Lent in the Western church

Easter is always preceded by a solemn season of religious observance known as Lent. It lasts for forty days in commemoration of the forty days Jesus spent fasting in the desert before he began his public ministry (see Matthew 4:1–11 and parallels).

In the Western church, Lent begins on Ash Wednesday, so called from the custom of placing ashes made from palm branches blessed on the previous Palm Sunday, on the heads of recipients while exhorting them to repent of their sins.

Many Christians commit to fasting or giving up certain luxuries as a form of penitence and self-denial, and may read a daily devotional for spiritual discipline. Churches often remove flowers from their altars and cover religious symbols. The service of the Stations of the Cross, a devotional re-enactment of Christ's Passion, is often observed. The liturgical colour for Lent is purple.

The season includes several significant dates:

- The fourth Sunday which marks the halfway point between Ash Wednesday and Easter Sunday, is known as Laetare Sunday (laetare is a Latin word meaning 'rejoice'). As on Gaudete Sunday in Advent, priests have the option of wearing rose-coloured vestments instead of purple.

- The fourth Sunday is also known as Mothering Sunday. It has recently become an occasion for honouring mothers of children, but has its origin in a 16th-century celebration of the Mother church.

- The fifth Sunday, known as Passion Sunday; the beginning of Passiontide.

- The sixth Sunday, known as Palm Sunday, marks the beginning of Holy Week, the final week of Lent immediately preceding Easter. It commemorates Jesus' triumphant entry into Jerusalem a week before his crucifixion.

Specification content

Easter The similarities (with reference to the doctrine of the resurrection of Christ) and differences (date; liturgical practice at Easter; the diversity within each stream of tradition) between the Eastern Orthodox and the Western churches' celebration of Easter.

quickfire

4.14 Why is Easter the most important of all Christian festivals?

quickfire

4.15 Why does the season of Lent last for forty days?

Key terms

Laetare Sunday: the fourth Sunday in Lent; also known as Mothering Sunday

Lent: in the Christian calendar, the period of forty days preparation for Easter

Palm Sunday: the sixth Sunday in Lent; commemorates Jesus' triumphant entry into Jerusalem and marks the beginning of Holy Week

Passion Sunday: the fifth Sunday in Lent; marks the start of the commemoration of Jesus' Passion

The Jewish Passover: the Jewish festival commemorating the Exodus

Vernal equinox: the time (around 21 March) when the sun crosses the earth's equator, making night and day of approximately equal length all over the earth

Key quote

Faith in the resurrection of Jesus says that there is a future for every human being; the cry for unending life which is a part of the person is indeed answered ... God exists: that is the real message of Easter. Anyone who even begins to grasp what this means also knows what it means to be redeemed. (Pope Benedict XVI)

Key quote

When He had fasted for forty days and forty nights, and afterwards was hungry, He gave an opportunity to the devil to draw near, so that He might teach us through this encounter how we are to overcome and defeat him ... For, desiring to draw the devil into contest, He made His hunger known to him. He met him as he approached, and meeting him, with the skill which He alone possessed, He once, twice, and a third time, threw His enemy to the ground. (St John Chrysostom)

- Thursday of Holy Week is known as Maundy Thursday or Holy Thursday, and is a day Christians commemorate the Last Supper shared by Christ with his disciples. As part of the celebration, the priest may wash the feet of twelve members of the congregation to commemorate Jesus' washing the disciples' feet (John 13:1–20).
- The next day is Good Friday, the day of atonement, on which Christians remember Jesus' crucifixion, death, and burial.
  - The Roman Catholic Church treats Good Friday as a fast day. There is no celebration of the Eucharist between Maundy Thursday and the Easter Vigil, but Holy Communion is distributed from the reserved sacrament. The only sacraments celebrated are baptism (for those in danger of death), penance and anointing of the sick. The celebration of the Passion of the Lord takes place usually at 3.00 pm and the vestments used are black or red. The Stations of the Cross are often prayed either in church or outside.
  - The Anglican Communion does not observe a particular rite on Good Friday but a popular service is the three-hour Meditation on the Cross that begins at 12.00 pm.
  - In the Lutheran Church the Good Friday liturgy is part of the one liturgy of the Holy Tridium (Maundy Thursday, Good Friday, Easter Vigil) which commemorates the death and resurrection of Jesus. A popular custom is to celebrate a *Tenebrae* service on Good Friday, which is held by candlelight and consists of passion accounts from the four Gospels.

Easter in the Western church

A Vigil may be held after nightfall on Holy Saturday or before dawn on Easter Sunday, when a paschal candle symbolising the resurrection of Jesus is lit. Statues and images that may have been veiled during Lent are unveiled.

Easter Day in the Western church is a joyous celebration of Christ's resurrection. In stark contrast to the solemnity of Lent, the liturgical colour is white, often with gold, and churches are brightly decorated with white and yellow flowers. The music is joyful and there is jubilant use of church bells.

Lent in the Eastern church

In the Eastern Orthodox Church, Easter is preceded by the most important fasting season in the church year, known as Great Lent or the Great Fast. Great Lent itself is preceded by a three-week period of preparation, and is followed by Holy Week leading up to Easter Day.

The first week of Great Lent starts not on Ash Wednesday but on Clean Monday. The name Clean Week refers to the spiritual cleansing of the faithful. Throughout this week there is strict fasting. The second week commemorates St Gregory Palamas, one of the great saints of the Orthodox Church. On the Sunday of the third week – the midpoint of the Great Fast – the Veneration of he Cross is celebrated. During an all-night Vigil the priest brings a cross out into the centre of the church, where it is venerated by all. The fourth week is an extension of the Veneration of the Cross. Saturday of the fifth week is dedicated to the *Theotokos* (Mother of God), and is known as *Akathist Saturday*, because a hymn to Mary is sung during Matins, with everyone standing (à-,'not' + *káthisis*, 'sitting'). Great Lent ends with Vespers on the Friday of the sixth week, and is followed by Lazarus Saturday, which celebrates the resuscitation of Lazarus as a foreshadowing of the resurrection of Jesus.

Holy Week services begin on the night of Palm Sunday. The blessing of palms takes place at Matins on Sunday morning.

During Holy Week, each day has its own theme:

- *Holy and Great Monday*: Joseph as a type of Christ; the Cursing of the Fig Tree.
- *Holy and Great Tuesday*: the Parable of the Ten Virgins.
- *Holy and Great Wednesday*: the anointing of Jesus at Bethany.
- *Holy and Great Thursday*: the Mystical Supper. This is a more festive day than the others because it celebrates the institution of the Eucharist.
- *Holy and Great Friday*: Jesus' Passion. This is a strict fast day. There are morning, afternoon and evening services of great solemnity. The evening service includes Lamentation Praises which reflect Mary's lament for her son. A cloth icon, known as the *epitaphios*, representing the sheet in which Jesus was buried, is placed on an ornate bier representing Jesus' tomb. The priest then sprinkles the tomb with rose water and fresh rose petals.
- *Holy and Great Saturday*: Jesus' Burial and his Descent into Hell. Another day of strict fasting. Services combine elements of sorrow and joy. At the beginning of the morning service, the liturgical colour is still black, but just before the Gospel reading it is changed to white and the atmosphere of the service turns from sorrow to joy. The priest sprinkles the church with fresh bay leaves to symbolise Jesus' victory over death. His salvific work has now been accomplished. The good news of his resurrection has, however, will only be proclaimed during the Paschal Vigil.

> **Key term**
>
> **Paschal Vigil:** The Easter service that is the first official celebration of the Resurrection of Jesus. Also called Easter Vigil.

Easter in the Eastern church

The last liturgical service in the Eastern Lent is the Midnight Office, which forms the first part of the Paschal Vigil. During this service the priest places the *epitaphios* on the altar, where it will remain until the feast of the Ascension. At the end of the Office, all church lights and candles are extinguished, and all wait in silence and darkness for the stroke of midnight, when the resurrection of Christ is proclaimed.

At midnight, the priest lights a candle. He then lights candles held by assistants, who in turn light candles held by the congregation. They all then process around the church chanting, 'At thy resurrection O Christ our Saviour, the angels in Heaven sing, enable us who are on earth, to glorify thee in purity of heart'.

The procession halts in front of the closed doors of the church, where the priest makes the sign of the cross and all church bells and percussion instruments are sounded. Then, Easter Matins begin, followed by the Easter Hours and the Easter Divine Liturgy.

Easter Vigil in an Eastern Orthodox church

Following the Liturgy, the priest may bless paschal eggs and baskets containing foods forbidden during the Great Fast, and the congregation may share an *agápē* meal. It is also customary to crack open hard-boiled eggs, dyed red to symbolise the blood of Christ, to celebrate the opening of Jesus' tomb.

On Easter Sunday afternoon *Agápē Vespers* are sung. During this service a portion of the Gospel of John may be read in several languages to demonstrate the universality of the resurrection.

Easter week is known as 'Bright Week'. There is no fasting. The customary Easter greeting is: 'Christ is risen', and the response is: 'He is risen indeed'.

Key skills

Knowledge involves:

Selection of a range of (thorough) accurate and relevant information that is directly related to the specific demands of the question.

This means you choose the correct information relevant to the question set NOT the topic area. You will have to think and focus on selecting key information and NOT writing everything you know about the topic area.

Understanding involves:

Explanation that is extensive, demonstrating depth and/or breadth with excellent use of evidence and examples including (where appropriate) thorough and accurate supporting use of sacred texts, sources of wisdom and specialist language.

This means that you demonstrate that you understand something by being able to illustrate and expand your points through examples/supporting evidence in a personal way and NOT repeat chunks from a text book (known as rote learning).

Further application of skills:

Go through the topic areas in this section and create some bullet lists of key points from key areas. For each one, provide further elaboration and explanation through the use of evidence and examples.

AO1 Developing skills

It is now time to reflect upon the information that has been covered so far. It is also important to consider how what you have learned can be focused and used for examination-style answers by practising the skills associated with AO1.

Assessment objective 1 (AO1) involves demonstrating knowledge and understanding. The terms 'knowledge' and 'understanding' are obvious but it is crucial to be familiar with how certain skills demonstrate these terms, and also, how the performance of these skills is measured (see generic band descriptors Band 5 for AS AO1).

You are now nearing the end of this section of the course. From now on the task will have only instructions with no examples; however, using the skills you have developed in completing the earlier tasks, you should be able to apply what you have learned to do and complete this successfully.

▶ **Your new task is this:** you will have to write another response under timed conditions to a question requiring an examination of how Great Lent, or the Great Fast, is celebrated in the Eastern Orthodox Church. You will need to do the same as your last AO1 Developing skills task but with some further development. This time there is a fifth point to help you improve the quality of your answers.

1. **Begin with a list of indicative content. Perhaps discuss this as a group. It does not need to be in any order.**

2. **Develop the list using examples.**

3. **Now consider in which order you would like to explain the information.**

4. **Then write out your plan, under timed conditions, remembering the principles of explaining with evidence and/ or examples.**

5. **Use the band descriptors to mark your own answer, considering carefully the descriptors. Then ask someone else to read your answer and see if then can help you improve it in any way.**

Use this technique as revision for each of the topic areas that you have studied. Swap and compare answers to improve your own.

Issues for analysis and evaluation

Whether the different emphases and practices mean that Easter is a different celebration in the Eastern Orthodox and Western churches

Specification content

Whether the different emphases and practices mean that Easter is a different celebration in the Eastern Orthodox and Western churches.

While they agree on the formula for setting the date of Easter, in most years Western and Eastern Orthodox churches celebrate the festival on different dates. This is because they use different calendars and have different interpretations of what is meant by the vernal equinox and the full moon. The Eastern church also insists that Easter should fall after the Jewish Passover.

Easter is preceded by the forty-day season of Lent. In the Wetsern church, Lent begins on Ash Wednesday. In the Eastern church, it begins on Clean Monday, and there is much more emphasis on strict fasting than in the Western church.

The pre-Easter season of Lent includes several significant dates, but they are different in both churches. For example, in the Western church, the Sunday which marks the halfway point between Ash Wednesday and Easter Sunday is traditionally known as Laetare Sunday. More recently it has become a celebration of motherhood (Mothering Sunday). The Eastern church celebrates the Veneration of the Cross on this day. Again, the Eastern church has a different theme for each day of Holy Week, whereas the Western church celebrates only Maundy Thursday, Good Friday and Holy Saturday.

While some Western churches may hold a Vigil after nightfall on Holy Saturday or before dawn on Easter Sunday, the main Easter celebration is on Easter Day. In the Eastern church, however, the main Easter celebration is an all-night service including the Paschal Vigil, leading to Easter Matins, the Easter Hours and the Easter Divine Liturgy. Following the Liturgy, the priest may bless hard-boiled eggs, dyed red to symbolise the blood of Christ, to celebrate the opening of Jesus' tomb.

Both Eastern and Western churches consider Easter to be the most important festival in the Christian calendar because it celebrates the fundamental Christian belief in the resurrection. They prepare carefully for it and celebrate it joyously and jubilantly.

For some Western churches there is some time given over in Easter services specifically for baptisms and the renewing of baptismal vows. For some Eastern churches, in the church at midnight all light is extinguished and then a new flame is struck at the altar. From that light, as everybody holds a candle, the light gradually spreads outwards to indicate Jesus, as light of the world, returning from the darkness of death.

It is not certain how far it could be argued that the emphasis of Easter in either tradition is more on resurrection than of death since both traditions seem to hold the two elements equally central. For example, both see Good Friday as austere with Lent as a preparation.

It could be concluded that there is not really a great deal of difference. The main differences within Christianity would be with the Christian groups that do not celebrate it at all.

AO2 Activity *Possible lines of argument*

Listed below are some conclusions that could be drawn from the AO2 reasoning in the above text:

1. Different emphases and practices mean that Easter is a different celebration in the Eastern Orthodox and Western churches.

2. Different emphases and practices make little difference to the basc celebration of Easter in the Eastern Orthodox and Western churches.

3. Different emphases and practices enhance the Eastern Orthodox and Western churches' shared understanding of Easter.

Consider each of the conclusions drawn above and collect evidence and examples to support each argument from the AO1 and AO2 material studied in this section. Select one conclusion that you think is most convincing and explain why it is so. Now contrast this with the weakest conclusion in the list, justifying your argument with clear reasoning and evidence.

The relative importance of Easter and Christmas

Traditionally, the most important Christian festival is Easter, but Christmas has in recent years seemed to surpass Easter, especially in the West.

Easter has always taken precedence because it celebrates the fundamental Christian belief in the resurrrection of Jesus Christ by which God set his seal of approval on his work. Without the resurrection, there is no hope of eternal life and Christian faith, as Paul famously said, 'is in vain'.

Christmas celebrates the birth of Christ, the incarnation (God becoming flesh). This too is an important celebration. It heralds the life, work and death of Jesus. Without the incarnation, of course, there could have been no resurrection.

The popularity of Christmas, however, often has little to do with Christian belief. The festival is open to several interpretations as 'the children's festival', 'the festival of peace' or even 'the mid-winter festival', based on the ancient Roman saturnalia, which it replaced. In the West, it has in recent years been heavily secularised and commercialised. While most people of all faiths and none may have some idea what the Christian celebration is about, and may often share in carol singing and charity fund raising at this time, belief in the incarnation may well be confined to a minority. The festival's popularity, however, is itself an opportunity for evangelisation.

There is perhaps less scope to re-interpret Easter, although it is often pointed out that the Christian festival originally replaced an ancient spring festival heralding the re-birth of nature (the English word Easter is derived from the name of an Anglo-Saxon spring goddess, *Ēostre*). In the West, there has been in recent years a relentless attempt to secularise and commercialise Easter too, with an emphasis on non-Christian imagery such as Easter bunnies. Again, while most people of all faiths and none may be willing to share Easter eggs, few may know that they are intended as symbols of the resurrection, and fewer still may believe in the resurrection itself. There is here too, however, an opportuinity for evangelisation.

For Christians, both festivals are important. They show God breaking into his world first as an innocent infant in the person of Jesus (the incarnation), and then as a mighty power raising the dead Jesus to life (the resurrection). The resurrection guarantees that God has accepted Jesus' death as an acceptable atonement for human sin, thus making eternal life possible for human beings.

In conclusion, it may be argued that Easter more important because it is about his ultimate mission rather than just his birth. Without Easter, Christmas would be insignificant since it would just be about a birth of a good teacher that had little significance, if the death and resurrection of Jesus are not true.

Whilst Christmas is a late addition to Church celebrations, Easter is not. Easter is more focused, sombre and religious, whilst Christmas because it is more joyful is much more popular. It could, however, be argued that of the two festivals, Christmas is the one that has lost its real religious significance and meaning. After all, Christmas cards are widespread but rarely religious!

AO2 Activity *Possible lines of argument*

Listed below are some conclusions that could be drawn from the AO2 reasoning in the above text:

1. Easter is a more important Christian festival than Christmas.

2. Christmas is a more important Christian festival than Easter.

3. Christmas and Easter are equally important Christian festivals.

Consider each of the conclusions drawn above and collect evidence and examples to support each argument from the AO1 and AO2 material studied in this section. Select one conclusion that you think is most convincing and explain why it is so. Now contrast this with the weakest conclusion in the list, justifying your argument with clear reasoning and evidence.

AO2 Developing skills

It is now time to reflect upon the information that has been covered so far. It is also important to consider how what you have learned can be focused and used for examination-style answers by practising the skills associated with AO2.

Assessment objective 2 (AO2) involves 'analysis' and 'evaluation'. The terms may be obvious but it is crucial to be familiar with how certain skills demonstrate these terms, and also, how the performance of these skills is measured (see generic band descriptors Band 5 for AS AO2).

Obviously an answer is placed within an appropriate band descriptor depending upon how well the answer performs, ranging from excellent, good, satisfactory, basic/limited to very limited.

You are now nearing the end of this section of the course. From now on the task will have only instructions with no examples; however, using the skills you have developed in completing the earlier tasks, you should be able to apply what you have learned to do and complete this successfully.

▶ **Your new task is this:** you will have to write another response under timed conditions to a question requiring an evaluation of whether or not Christmas is a more important Christian festival than Easter. You will need to do the same as your last AO2 Developing skills task but with some further development. This time there is a fifth point to help you improve the quality of your answers.

1. **Begin with a list of indicative content. Perhaps discuss this as a group. It does not need to be in any order. Remember, this is evaluation, so you need different lines of argument. The easiest way is to use the 'support' and 'against' headings.**

2. **Develop the list using examples.**

3. **Now consider in which order you would like to explain the information.**

4. **Then write out your plan, under timed conditions, remembering to apply the principles of evaluation by making sure that you: identify issues clearly; present accurate views of others making sure that you comment on the views presented; reach an overall personal judgement.**

5. **Use the band descriptors to mark your own answer, considering carefully the descriptors. Then ask someone else to read your answer and see if then can help you improve it in any way.**

Use this technique as revision for each of the topic areas that you have studied. Swap and compare answers to improve your own.

Key skills

Analysis involves identifying issues raised by the materials in the AO1, together with those identified in the AO2 section, and presents sustained and clear views, either of scholars or from a personal perspective ready for evaluation.

This means that it picks out key things to debate and the lines of argument presented by others or a personal point of view.

Evaluation involves considering the various implications of the issues raised based upon the evidence gleaned from analysis and provides an extensive detailed argument with a clear conclusion.

This means that the answer weighs up the various and different lines of argument analysed through individual commentary and response and arrives at a conclusion through a clear process of reasoning.

Questions and answers

Theme 1

AO1 question area: *Examining how Bultmann interprets the early church's belief in Jesus' resurrection.*

A strong answer

Rudolf Bultmann was a twentieth-century German theologian who argued that there was a need to 'demythologise' the New Testament in order to present its message in terms acceptable to modern readers. [1]

Bultmann defined 'myth' as 'the report of an event or occurrence in which supernatural, superhuman powers or persons are at work'. In the New Testament, he classified as myth the story of Jesus' resurrection. It is, he argued, a story designed to sustain faith. The resurrection was not a historical event, and scientifically minded modern readers cannot be expected to believe that it was. [2]

In fact, Bultmann says, belief in the resurrection of Jesus' physical body is not only unnecessary to Christian faith but also contrary to faith. 'Faith,' according to the Epistle to the Hebrews, 'is the assurance of things hoped for'. [3] There is no need, therefore, for faith in historical facts. What is important, wrote Bultmann, is that Jesus 'is alive again if you see him as such with the eyes of faith'.

The disciples certainly saw him so. According to Bultmann, the disciples, following Jesus' death, suddenly realised that he was the Son of God. This had to mean that, having suffered death, God had conquered death. The alternative was that death had conquered God, and that made no sense. [4] The Christian faith originates not from the rising of Jesus but from the rise of this belief in the disciples.

The victory over death comes, therefore, through Jesus' cross. There was no need for the resurrection as a historical event. The crucifixion contained the resurrection within it. As Bultmann puts it in his book, *Kerygma and Myth*, 'Faith in the resurrection is really the same thing as faith in the saving efficacy of the Cross'. [5]

'Faith in the saving efficacy of the Cross' is kindled by listening to 'the word of preaching'. The resurrection takes place within individuals as they hear the word of preaching and experience the rise of faith. It is through preaching, not through any historical resurrection event that people are saved.

For Bultmann, therefore, the crucifixion and resurrection of Jesus are not two events but one, and belief in the resurrection can only come about through faith. [6]

Commentary

1. The introductory paragraph shows that the candidate knows who Bultmann was.
2. The second paragraph defines 'myth' and why it is unacceptable to modern readers.
3. There is evidence here of reading outside this textbook – something that is always credited.
4. The reasoning behind the belief in Jesus' alleged conquest of death is convincingly explained.
5. An appropriate quote, correct, complete and identified.
6. The essay content is aptly summarised in a relevant conclusion.

Summative comment

This is a very well-structured and clearly expressed answer with some good detail in terms of defining, evidencing and explaining Bultmann's work and his specific interpretation of the early church's belief in Jesus' resurrection.

AO2 question area: *Evaluating the extent to which Bultmann's theology is helpful to Christians today.*

A weak answer

There is no doubt at all that Bultmann's theology is not always helpful today. [1] Twenty-first century Christians live in a world of science and technology, and do not share the New Testament writers' mythological worldview. Modern Christians cannot be expected to believe in such things as Jesus' virgin birth, his miracles and his resurrection.

Some say this is why Bultmann's theology is helpful. To strip the New Testament of all its mythological elements about angels, miraculous healings and people being raised from the dead is to make it more accessible to the modern reader. [2]

But some people today like all the supernatural elements and believe in them. [3] Others argue that people today must be given a more credible presentation of Jesus' divinity. Bultmann's theory that Jesus' divinity was revealed to the disciples following his death on the cross is such a presentation.

After all, what matters is not whether or not Jesus rose physically from the dead two thousand years ago, but that he has arisen today in people's hearts. Some people have criticised Bultmann's theology. [4] But surely he was right about this? He has made the Christian faith relevant to our educated and sophisticated age.

Commentary

1 The candidate has reached a conclusion before beginning to answer the question. This is alright as long as what follows it ties in with the reasoning.

2 It is obvious that the candidate knows what Bultmann's theology is about, but the technical word *demythologisation* is not used.

3 A decent counter-argument but it is not developed.

4 This statement needs developing. The answer does not put any arguments against the contention. This is a major weakness and it does not link in with the conclusion it started with!

Summative comment

The answer understands the main debate but it is confusing and does not have a clear line of argument. The suggestion that it is not helpful is asserted and not really developed. Not the worst answer but nowhere near the best.

Theme 2

AO1 question area: *Examining Sallie McFague's understanding of God.*

A weak answer

Sallie McFague is an American ecofeminist theologian. She has developed three new metaphors for God. 1

The first is God as Mother. This corresponds to the traditional title of God the Father. It is associated with the doctrine of creation, the idea of justice and also with *agape* love.

The second is God as Loving. This corresponds to the traditional title of God the Son. It is associated with the doctrine of salvation, the idea of healing, and with *erons* (desire).

The third is God as Friend. 2 This corresponds to the traditional idea of God the Holy Spirit. It is associated with the doctrine of eschatology; the idea of companionship; and *filina* (the way in which humans should interact in the world). 3

McFague thinks that it might influence people to look after the earth if they thought of God as a Mother who cares for the world rather than as a Father who thinks he can lord it over everything. 4

However, in relation to Jesus, the terms Father and Mother are not interchangeable, because Jesus referred to God as 'Father', and his mother was clearly Mary. 5

Commentary

1 There is no definition of what 'ecofeminism' is. It would have been good to establish this at the outset.

2 There is obvious awareness of some of McFague's ideas. However, the metaphors of God as Lover and Friend are not relevant to the question.

3 There are one or two errors here: the second aspect is God as 'Lover' not 'Loving'; the Greek word for desire is eros not erons; and, the word for friendship love in Greek is philia not filina. Be careful with use of technical and religious terminology. Be precise!

4 This paragraph is fine as far as it goes, but it needs development. It has nothing on God's care, justice and love.

5 The answer ends abruptly with a criticism of 'ecofeminism' that is not relevant to the question.

Summative comment

This answer has the basics of understanding of 'ecofeminism' but little more to offer. There could have been much more development of the definition, the main ideas and examples and evidence to back up the ecofeminist point of view are clearly lacking.

AO2 question area: *Evaluating whether or not it is entirely valid for a Christian to speak of God as Mother.*

A strong answer

Influenced by modern feminist theology, 21st-century Christianity increasingly speaks of God as Mother. 1 Many people think that this is entirely valid. The biblical concept of God as Father is patriarchal language, which shapes our image of God. This in turn shapes our relationship with God and other people. It follows that if men think of God only in terms of 'fatherly' characteristics, such as power and authority, they are likely to exploit women and to abuse the earth. 2

God's nature has no gender, but it embodies feminine characteristics, such as compassion, grace, love, which are equally important as the masculine characteristics of redeeming, administering justice, and establishing peace.

The Bible contains several female images of God. In the Old Testament, Isaiah describes God as a comforting mother. In the New Testament, Jesus compares God to a woman searching for a lost coin. This image of God as sustainer and healer is not just scriptural: it is part of people's life experience. 3

Others, however, would reject this view on the grounds that there is no biblical precedent for referring to God as Mother. In the Bible God chose to reveal his identity in masculine language, which tells us something about his nature and character as creator, provider, etc. Nonetheless, this should be seen in the patriarchal context and is not really a strong argument to use on its own because it was clearly written by men for men. **4**

While there is some female imagery for God in the Bible, it is rare and there are no feminine names or titles for God. God is never called 'queen', for example, or 'wife'.

Most importantly, Jesus used the term 'Father'. It conveys his Father–Son relationship with God, which is eternal. Again, this only serves to underline the gender bias of the Bible and is there any good reason why a Father–Son relationship would be better than a more neutral relationship with a parent figure? **5**

Moreover, the concept of God as Mother of the world is suspect as it brings to mind ancient Near Eastern cults where the mother-goddess gives birth to the earth. However, whilst this is an argument that clarifies why the Bible may have a male focus on God here, this does not mean that this is relevant today. **6**

In conclusion, the concept of God as Mother has raised some controversy, but has proven helpful to many and is gaining increasing validity in Christian circles. There are arguments still presented against it; however, they are not strong enough to resist the challenge of God as Mother. Anyway, does it have to be one or the other or can we look forward to a day in which Christianity may embrace both understandings as useful for developing our understanding of the Christian God? **7**

Commentary

1. The matter under consideration is neatly introduced.

2. A good explanation of the rationale behind the approach.

3. Two strong arguments are made in favour of the contention, namely: God's feminine characteristics; biblical female images of God. Both are presented well.

4. A brief counter-argument is recognised, that of no biblical precedent. Examples could have been given but it was good to identify a possible response to this and identify and evaluate the argument's weakness.

5. There is now another counter-argument using Jesus and his relationship to the Father as an example and another good evaluation of it.

6. The unsuitability of the Mother image as an argument is allowed but evaluated well and contextualised.

7. The answer ends with an appropriate conclusions and a very good question posed indicating independent thought.

Summative comment

A very mature and thoughtful response with strong evaluative elements and a strong line of independent reasoning throughout.

Theme 3

AO1 question area: *Examining what is meant by justification by faith alone.*

A weak answer

In the Middle Ages, the Roman Catholic Church taught that Christians who died without having done adequate penance for their sins had to spend time in a place of suffering called purgatory before being accepted into heaven. **1** However, living people could free their dead relatives from purgatory by buying an official piece of paper known as an indulgence. A popular jingle of the time said 'As soon as a coin in the coffer rings / the soul from purgatory springs'. The money raised went towards building a new church in Rome. **2**

Martin Luther, a German monk, was appalled at this practice. Luther was a godly man who had been plagued by an overwhelming sense of his own sinfulness. Despite doing everything that the church asked of him – praying, confessing his sins and doing penance – he had felt that he was losing touch with God. Then, he read Paul's statement that the 'righteous will live by faith alone' **3** , and realised that God was not asking him to do anything other than believe in Jesus. From this he developed his doctrine of *sola fide*, 'by faith alone' – that all people need do in order to receive salvation is to have faith in God's promise of forgiveness. **4**

There were some passages in the New Testament that contradicted Luther's doctrine, but Luther dismissed these as having nothing of the nature of the Gospel about them. **5** In October 1517, he published his Ninety-five Theses against clerical abuses in the Roman Catholic Church. This was the spark that ignited the Protestant Reformation.

Commentary

1. The opening statement is about the doctrine of purgatory, not about the doctrine of *sola fide*.

2. This is not strictly accurate: (a) Freeing of dead relatives from purgatory through purchase of an indulgence was not Catholic teaching. It was a distortion preached by Tetzel. (b) Half the proceeds of the sales of indulgences in the archbishopric of Mainz in Germany went to the Cardinal Archbishop.

3. The reference to Paul's statement is vague and does not specify where it occurs. It is also inaccurate because Paul does not use the word 'alone'.

4. This is accurate but could have been developed and is not a full explanation.

5. Another vague reference to passages 'that contradicted Luther's doctrine'. Where are they, and what do they say?

Summative comment

The response addresses the question, but is patchy, and unfocused demonstrating only some understanding of the main idea of *sola fide*. There is a lack of development and depth because the first and last sections are not really made relevant to the focus of the answer.

AO2 question area: *Evaluating whether or not the Council of Trent's response to justification by faith alone was convincing.*

A strong answer

The Council of Trent was held from 1545 to 1563 to consider the Roman Catholic Church's response to the Protestant Reformation that had been triggered off by Luther in 1517. [1]

On the subject of *sola fide*, the Council pronounced in 1547 that justification is not simply the gift of God. People must become righteous, and good works are required as a condition. People cannot, however, bring about their own justification. They must cooperate with the grace of God. Justification works in two phases. Initial justification is by grace, which is God's gift mediated through baptism. Thereafter, justification depends on participation in the Eucharist and doing good works. Justification, therefore, is a matter not of faith alone, but of faith and works. [2]

Some people would argue that this view is convincing because it is biblical. Nowhere in the Bible does it say that people are justified by faith *alone*. In fact, the Epistle of James states clearly that people are *not* justified by faith alone. Trent balances James' statement, and others by Paul (e.g. in Romans, 'the doers of the law ... will be justified) with the Pauline doctrine that 'the righteous will live by faith'. Trent's view thus protects against the heresy of antinomianism (the belief that faith is all that is required and that God's laws may be ignored) and gives sinners a certain amount of responsibility for their salvation. If Trent is correct, justification depends not only on being declared righteous by God through baptism, but also on perseverance in good works. There can be no salvation without human effort. [3]

Others would argue that Trent's view is not convincing. There are biblical grounds to support the doctrine that God simply acquits sinners of guilt. There is an example in Psalm 32:2: 'Happy are those to whom the Lord imputes no iniquity'. In the New Testament, the doctrine is developed to maintain that God imputes to sinners the righteousness of Jesus. As Paul writes in II Corinthians, 'in Christ God was reconciling the world to himself, not counting their trespasses against them'. Justification is thus a declarative act of God's grace. It does not, however, exempt believers from doing good works. Christians perform good works not that they may be justified, but because they have been justified. Good works do not produce righteousness. It is righteousness that produces good works. [4]

The conflict over the nature of justification was one of the root causes of the Protestant Reformation. In 1999, however, the Roman Catholic Church and the Lutheran World Federation agreed a Joint Declaration on the subject. In 2008, Pope Benedict XVI declared that 'Being just simply means being with Christ, being in Christ, that is all ... Luther's expression *sola fide* is true, if faith is not against charity, against love.' It is clear that this declaration serves to pacify the two extremes of the original debate that has lasted hundreds of years; however, it is clear that whilst faith alone is true, the most obvious way of acting upon that faith is the natural expression of good works through Christian love. [5]

Commentary

[1] The first paragraph explains succinctly what the Council of Trent was and when it was held.

[2] Paragraph 2 explains what Trent decided on *sola fide*.

[3] Paragraph 3 sets out a case in favour of the contention, focusing on two arguments – that Trent's decision was based on biblical evidence and that it guarded against the heresy of antinomianism.

[4] Paragraph 4 sets out an equally strong case against the contention, focusing on biblical evidence and quoting a verse from the Psalms which demonstrates individual research.

[5] The final paragraph is an appropriate conclusion, again showing commendable evidence of reading outside the text of this book. The overall response is thorough, analysing and evaluating different views.

Summative comment

An excellent answer demonstrating a strong use of evidence and explanation of arguments in relation to the statement. A great deal of detail is included.

Theme 4

AO1 question area: *Examining the case for infant baptism as put forward by Augustine.*

A strong answer

Augustine argued the case for infant baptism. He wrote that it was a 'tradition received from the apostles' as a means of removing original sin. According to The Council of Carthage in 418 CE 'even babies, who are yet unable to commit any sin personally, are truly baptised for the forgiveness of sins'. **1**

Augustine based his argument on bilical evidence such as that found in John 3:5, where Jesus tells Nicodemus: 'I tell you, no one can enter the kingdom of God without being born of water and Spirit'. His words include infants. Also, in Acts 2:38–39: Peter said to them, 'Repent, and be baptised every one of you in the name of Jesus Christ so that your sins may be forgiven; and you will receive the gift of the Holy Spirit. For the promise is for you, for your children.' **2**

As well as this, it was familiar practice in Acts for the Apostles to baptise all households which obviously included infants. Indeed, many Christians see baptism as the Christian equivalent to 'a spiritual circumcision' (Colossians 2:11–12). Christians are 'buried with' Jesus in baptism and 'raised with him through faith in the power of God'. **3**

Infant baptism was practised throughout the early church, and was supported by all the church Fathers, specifically Augustine. Augustine wrote a lot about infant baptism, which he argued was something that the universal church had 'always held', and was 'most correctly believed to have been handed down by apostolic authority'. **4**

Augustine believed baptised infants were not able to imitate Christ but because they are 'ingrafted' into his body, then, Christ gives to believers the grace of his Spirit, 'which he secretly infuses even into infants'. For Augustine, Christ could never exclude infants. **5**

Even though infants are not able to profess a personal faith, the church should still baptise them, according to Augustine who argued, 'When children are presented to be given spiritual grace, it is not so much those holding them in their arms who present them ... as the whole company of saints and faithful Christians .... It is done by the whole of Mother Church'. For Augustine, baptised infants believe not on their own account, but 'through the Church's faith communicated to them'. **6**

For Augustine, baptism was a sacrament which means that it somehow gives over a gift of spiritual grace and referred to North African Christians of his time who called the sacrament of baptism 'salvation'. He argued that this idea of salvation through baptism from apostolic tradition which asserted that 'without baptism and participation at the table of our Lord it is impossible for anyone to attain either to the kingdom of God or to salvation and life eternal'. For Augustine baptism was not only a sacrament but a specific 'sacrament of regeneration'. **7**

Commentary

1 An excellent introduction clearly stating the position of Augustine and the early church.

2 Good illustration of how Augustine's view is grounded in the evidence from the Bible.

3 Further evidence from the practice of the very early church as depicted in Acts is offered as support for Augustine's case.

4 A clear demonstration that Augustine was not alone in his thoughts and that the early church Fathers supported him.

5 The idea that Christ would never exclude infants from his grace is acknowledged and well stated.

6 The justification for the community supporting an infant as a body of believers is crucial to Augustine's argument.

7 A key factor in Augustine's argument is in the regenerative power of baptism as a sacrament and this is important to include and good to finish with.

Summative comment

A very comprehensive answer using good evidence and references to support Augustine's position. It is very well explained and highly accurate, leaving no stone unturned!

AO2 question area: *Evaluating the extent to which infant baptism is just a symbolic act.*

A weak answer

Some argue that baptism is a symbol for forgiveness and it is simply a sign of this.

Also it is a symbol that the one baptised has been accepted into the Christian church and belongs to the new covenant. [1]

Some also see it like a dramatic performance of the death, burial and resurrection of Jesus and see the power of water as an image to be like Noah's flood story that separates good from bad. [2]

However, Augustine argued that there is power in baptism because it regenerates a person so it cannot be just a symbol. [3]

In addition, if it was just a symbol it could not be a sacrament for Augustine. [4]

In conclusion, I think it is a symbol that has power and so both views are right. [5]

Commentary

[1] This is actually quite good in terms of the key points but there is no real development of them, nor any personal evaluation or commentary.

[2] There is no real support or justification offered for such a view.

[3] Augustine's argument is weakened in that it is not fully presented. Much more could have been made of the reasoning behind this and some critique of it offered.

[4] This is not, as stated, strictly speaking true and raises questions as to the level of understanding in the answer of the issue debated.

[5] A very weak conclusion that does not really make sense because it is not linked in any way to the above reasoning. A little more explanation and justification may have salvaged it.

Summative comment

A poor response that just identifies some key reasons for and against. There is also no reference to today's practices, which may have helped, no quotations or citations from scholars, which makes it weak overall.

Quickfire answers

Theme 1

1.1 The books of Micah, 2 Samuel, Jeremiah, Hosea and, maybe, Judges.

1.2 Because Quirinius was not governor of Syria 'in the days of Herod'.

1.3 He wants to prove that Jesus is descended from King David and that he is the fulfilment of Old Testament prophecy.

1.4 The news of Jesus' birth is brought for the first time to poor shepherds. Jesus is born in a manger and the offering made by his parents at his presentation in the Temple (two turtle doves) is that of poor people.

1.5 A style of writing that repeats similar ideas in reverse sequence (ABCBA).

1.6 The inauguration of the church's mission.

1.7 'Feed my lambs', 'Tend my sheep', 'Feed my sheep'.

1.8 'Resuscitation' means returning to the same life as before; 'resurrection' means returning to life in a different form.

1.9 To remove mythical elements from a text.

1.10 Jesus rising to life within individuals as they hear the preaching of the Word.

1.11 It is more sharply focused: it will be an act of new creation involving the gift of a new body with different properties.

1.12 Because he had been raised from the dead.

1.13 Greek *tà biblía* = 'the books'.

1.14 The sin of Adam and Eve which all human beings inherit.

1.15 'For our instruction, so that … we might have hope.'

Theme 2

2.1 God as Creator; God as an approachable deity.

2.2 God's female characteristics are that God gives birth, feeds, nurtures and protects; 'feminine' virtues (e.g. sentimentalising motherhood) are often social constructs.

2.3 *Impassibility*: having no human feelings; *immutability*: unchangeable.

2.4 *The Crucified God*.

2.5 Atheism based on how the problem of suffering destroys belief in a benevolent God.

2.6 Adoptionism, Sabellianism, Arianism.

2.7 'and the Son'.

2.8 *Immanent Trinity*: what God is; *Economic Trinity*: what God does.

2.9 The Holy Spirit.

2.10 'Mode of being'.

2.11 The sin of Adam and Eve which all human beings inherit.

2.12 'Setting at one', 'reconciliation'.

2.13 *Expiation*: what Christ did on the cross; *propitiation*: the result of what Christ did on the cross.

2.14 Because it was based on the concept of God's honour rather than on that of God's justice.

2.15 Sacrifice, Ransom, Christus Victor, Satisfaction, Penal Substitution, Moral Example.

Theme 3

3.1 'Being made righteous in the sight of God.'

3.2 *sola fide.*

3.3 A piece of paper issued by the Pope which granted a sinner remission from penance for a payment.

3.4 First, righteousness is mediated through baptism; second, it is increased by doing good works.

3.5 Covenantal nomism.

3.6 'Proclamation'; the preaching of the apostles.

3.7 The Christian church.

3.8 'A visible sign of God's grace'.

3.9 Baptism and the Eucharist.

3.10 The Christian church is both a sign and an instrument of God's grace.

3.11 On God's laws.

3.12 Because God first loved them.

3.13 The Bible and the work of the Holy Spirit.

3.14 Seventy-seven times (or seventy times seven).

3.15 The forgiveness freely granted to sinners by God.

Theme 4

4.1 Original sin.

4.2 The apostles.

4.3 Circumcision.

4.4 'Rebaptiser'.

4.5 That it is 'coercive', 'not done in obedience' and not 'administered according to proper order'.

4.6 'Thanksgiving'.

4.7 The doctrine that the bread and the wine of the Eucharist, when consecrated by a priest, change into the actual body and blood of Jesus.

4.8 The doctrine that the body and blood of Christ co-exist with the consecrated bread and wine of the Eucharist.

4.9 Huldrych Zwingli.

4.10 Virtualism and receptionism.

4.11 Christmas and the parousia.

4.12 A service held in church early on Christmas morning, when groups of men sang carols to await the Eucharist at daybreak.

4.13 7 January.

4.14 It celebrates the resurrection, which is the most important Christian belief.

4.15 In commemoration of the forty days Jesus spent fasting in the desert before he began his public ministry

Glossary

Absolution: declaration by a priest that a person's sins have been forgiven

Adoptionism: the belief that Jesus was an ordinary man who became the Son of God only at his baptism

Advent: in the Western Christian calendar the four weeks leading up to Christmas

Annunciation: Gabriel's announcement to Mary

Apostle (from Greek apóstolos): 'one who is sent'), messenger, ambassador; the name given to those sent by Jesus to proclaim his good news

Arianism: the belief that Jesus was the highest of all created beings but not of the same substance as God

Aspersion: sprinkling water over an infant's head as a sign of baptism

Atonement: to make 'at one' or reconcile

Benedictus: the first word of Zechariah's Prophecy; Latin: *blessed*; the Prophecy begins: 'Blessed be the Lord God of Israel'

Betrothed: engaged to be married

Birth narratives: the account of Jesus' birth in the Gospels of Matthew and Luke

Chiasm: a style of writing that repeats similar ideas in reverse sequence (ABCBA)

Chronology: timing

Circumcision: a Jewish religious rite performed on male infants on the eighth day after birth to commemorate God's covenant with Abraham (Genesis 17)

Consubstantiation: the belief that the body and blood of Christ co-exist with the consecrated bread and wine of the Eucharist

Covenant: an agreement between God and his people

Covenantal nomism: God's election of the Jews as a chosen nation provided they obeyed his commandments

Demythologise: to eliminate mythical elements from a piece of writing

Deuterocanonical: a second list of sacred books considered to be genuine

Didache: a Greek word meaning 'teaching'; what the apostles taught

Docetism: the heresy that Jesus did not suffer on the cross because his body was not human

Ecofeminist: someone who is interested in both the environment and women's rights

Expiation: what Christ did on the cross – he paid the penalty for human sin

Filioque: Latin for 'and the Son'

Gaudete Sunday: the third Sunday of Advent

Gentiles: non-Jews

Good Friday: the Friday before Easter Sunday; commemorates Christ's crucifixion an his atonement for sinners

Gospel: the record of Jesus' life and teaching in the first four books of the New Testament

Historicity: historical accuracy

Holy Spirit: God as he is active in the world

Hypostatic union: the combination of the divine and human nature in the Person of Christ

Immersion: baptising by immersing the candidate's whole body in water

Immutability: unchangeable

Impassibility: having no human feelings

Incarnation: God becoming flesh in Jesus

Kenosis: Jesus 'emptying' himself

Kerygma: a Greek word meaning 'proclamation'; what the apostles preached

Laetare Sunday: the fourth Sunday in Lent; also known as Mothering Sunday

Lent: in the Christian calendar, the period of forty days preparation for Easter

Logos asarkos: Greek for 'the Word without flesh'; Barth's term for the Son before he became incarnate

Magi: Latin for 'wise men' – originally the word meant 'an oriental priest, learned in astrology'

Magnificat: the first word of Mary's song; Latin: *magnifies*; the Song begins: 'My soul magnifies the Lord'

Maundy Thursday: Thursday in Holy Week; commemorates the institution of the Lord's Supper

Memorialism: the belief that the consecrated bread and wine of the Eucharist are merely symbolic representations of Christ's body and blood

Messiah: the saviour of the Jews promised in the Old Testament

Metaphor: something that represents or is a symbol for something else

Moral principle: the basis of right and wrong

Nunc dimittis: the first two words of Simeon's Song; Latin: *now you are releasing*; the Song begins: 'Now you are releasing your son in peace'

Objective: factual; not based on personal belief

Omnibenevolent: all good

Omnipotent: all-powerful

Omniscient: all-knowing

Original sin: the sin of Adam and Eve, which all human beings inherit

Palm Sunday: the sixth Sunday in Lent; commemorates Jesus' triumphant entry into Jerusalem and marks the beginning of Holy Week

Panentheism: the belief that the universe is the visible part of God

Parousia: the Second Coming of Christ

Paschal Vigil: the Easter service that is the first official celebration of the Resurrection of Jesus. Also called Easter Vigil.

Passion Sunday: the fifth Sunday in Lent; marks the start of the commemoration of Jesus' Passion

Plygain: originally an impromptu Welsh language service, held early on Christmas morning, when groups of men sang carols to await the Eucharist at daybreak

Predestination: the belief that God has elected some people to be saved, but not others

Preincarnate: before the incarnation

Propitiation: the result of what Christ did on the cross – he averted God's wrath

Rabbinic: relating to the teachings of Jewish rabbis

Redaction criticism: the theory that New Testament writers altered existing material about Jesus to suit their own agenda

Resurrection: rising from the dead

Sabellianism: the belief that Jesus was divine but not human

Salvation: deliverance from God's judgement of sin

Saturnalia: an ancient Roman mid-winter festival in honour of the god, Saturn

Seinsweise: Barth's word for 'mode of being', which he uses instead of the usual word Person to refer to the three members of the Godhead

Subjective: personal belief; not based on facts

Supererogation: doing more than duty requires

The Enlightenment: an 18th-century philosophical movement based on reason, tolerance, liberty, etc.

The Jewish Passover: the Jewish festival commemorating the Exodus

The Nativity Fast: what corresponds to Advent in the Eastern Orthodox Church

The Pentecost experience: the pouring of the Holy Spirit on the apostles on the first Christian Pentecost, as described in Acts 2:1–13

Transfinalization: the belief that when the bread and wine are consecrated their purpose is changed, but not their substance

Transignification: the belief that Christ is sacramentally, but not physically, present in the consecrated bread and wine

Transubstantiation: the belief that the bread an wine of the Eucharist actually become the body and blood of Christ when consecrated by a priest

Vernal equinox: the time (around 21 March) when the sun crosses the earth's equator, making night and day of approximately equal length all over the earth

Virtualism: the belief that Christ's unique power (Latin *virtus*) is present in the consecrated bread and wine, but that this power is received only by the predestined elect

Index